"When birth certificates are given, this book should
for human happiness, an exercise in fertility, and a ball of light in your hand. Read and be
transformed."

> —Michael Modzelewski, Discovery Channel host, author, celebrity,
> frequent Oprah guest, and extreme adventurer

"*Bliss Conscious Communication,* I love it! Bless U, Bliss U!"

> —Ram Dass, spiritual teacher and author of the bestselling classics
> *Be Here Now* and *Be Love Now*

"Happyo's wisdom is deep. Deepak deep. She may even be deeper than Deepak . . . you
might call her Deeperpak."

> —Steve Bhaerman (AKA Swami Beyondananda), inspirational comedian,
> insightful author of humorous wit & coauthor of *Spontaneous Evolution* with Bruce Lipton

"I was delighted to feature Happy Oasis as one of "America's Happy 100" in my book *Happy
for No Reason.* In *Bliss Conscious Communication,* she shows us how deep and lasting
happiness is rooted in our thoughts and offers us easy steps to deepen our experience of
happiness, joy and bliss."

> —Marci Shimoff, #1 *NY Times* bestselling author of *Love for No Reason* and
> *Happy for No Reason*

"Guaranteed to raise your conversational kundalini, *Bliss Conscious Communication* is the
quintessential groundbreaking phenomenon that is giving birth to today's budding new field
of Blissology. . . . This could be the most important book you ever *WRITE!*"

> —Johnny Liberty, renaissance man & author of *Global Sovereign's Handbook*

"*Bliss Conscious Communication* is not only fun to read, this book is a call to action, to
discover the ecstasy of ethics as well as the uplifting, powerful results of being creatively
considerate and astonishingly polite. These pages are filled with recipes for shifting our
words to better reflect the possibility that life holds, and the robust opportunity for positive,
purposeful creation."

> —Kimberly Carter Gamble, producer, director & co-writer of the movie *THRIVE*

"The shift in our communication allows us the opportunity to co-create a shift in our world. *Bliss Conscious Communication* is not only a book that allows us to become aware of how we can shift our projection onto the world. It is also an invitation to co-create with awareness, joy, love and the beautiful state of being happy."

—don Miguel Ruiz Jr., best-selling author of *Living a Life of Awareness* & *The Five Levels of Attachment*

This is the best book we have ever read and "coauthored" with thousands of others for inspiration, self help, and the power of the spoken word. We highly recommend this Have-to-Read-in-Your-Lifetime-Book to our clients and community, not only to read but also to co-write, reread and rewrite. What a foundation of joyous sharing for families, church groups, high school, college, university, therapy, spiritual, and community gatherings! May you enjoy coauthoring this juicy, fun, promising, hopeful, and transformational book as much as we do."

—Reverend Kedar & Shelley St. John, founders & ministers of Maui's Temple of Peace

"Why enjoy ecstasy for a night when one can experience ecstasy for a lifetime? For the sake of harmony with humanity, may we all master the Blissiplines within this book."

—Mirabai Devi, author & spiritual teacher of South Africa and Kauai

"Happyo has gone where others must not fear to tread. Bliss is the new '10' – consummate elation - and Happy conveys this better than anyone. All of us would be wise to reach for bliss as a way to blend and bend in times of change. Bliss is not out of our reach. It is our natural way of being, and Happy is here to remind us that bliss our birthright."

—Stephanie Sutton-Flanagan, founder of Planet HeartWorks & chair of Flantech, guiding the work of her husband, Dr. Patrick Flanagan

"At last! A book about communicating for heaven's sake."

—Toni Toney, author of *Eco Diet*

" Happy Oasis is a vortex of delight whose years of meditation immersion has naturally led her toward expanded, bliss-radiating awareness. In 2003, the ground-breaking edition of *Bliss Conscious Communication* invited humanity to glimpse into Blissology. This second edition continues to deeply explore blissful living and how to share it with others. I highly recommend delving into it and the many Blissiplines within."

—Sarah McLean, founder of Mclean Meditation Institute & author of *Soul Centered*

"Beyond the realm of normal words . . . bliss-inducing and scrumtrulescent."

—Zander Hathaway, cofounder of The Well Tree

"Conscious communication transmutes duality into oneness. This book guides you to that quintessential reality. Enjoy!"

—Dr. Jacob Liberman, author of *Light: Medicine of the Future, Take Off Your Glasses and See & Wisdom From an Empty Mind*

"Happy inspires us to have a Blissipline wedding with our higher selves as we cosmically juggle the linguistics of this soulful journey, extracting the sprouting spirit of infinite possibilities to distribute high vibrational smiles while expanding the mental music she has offered up to the altar of our co-creativity. The art of Blissology is a key nutrient in the realm of youthing, harmony and vitality."

— Viktoras Kulvinskas, author of the best-seller, *Survival Into the 21ˢᵗ Century*

"*Bliss Conscious Communication* is worthy of memorizing and utilizing in our everyday lives. Practicing these Blissiplines opens the door for the highest to express through us. Thank you, Happyo, for writing such a powerful book and thank you, Resplendent Reader, for coauthoring it, thereby co-creating a more joy-filled world."

—Dr. Richard Anderson, author of *Cleanse & Purify Thyself*

"A promise of peace and a marvelous friend with whom to take flight."

—Edrees Sabawoon, philosopher, Afghanistan

"A delightful romp into the world of creative, positive, uplifting communication with awesome suggestions to banish mundane conversations forever via spreading the bliss!"

—Eric T. Richter, publisher, *Maui Vision Magazine*

In each generation we are given the medicine for the healing of our generation. *Bliss Conscious Communication* is the healing and liberating medicine of now for this generation."

— Rabbi Gabriel Cousens, author, M.D., M.D. (H.), D.D., founder of The Tree Of Life

"Don't just buy this book, grok it, and you will find bliss fields blooming in your mind and heart. The Blissipline Prophesy has been fulfilled with this publication. Read at your own blissk."

—Tony Carito, Sedona's most celebrated inspirational comedian

Read more rave reviews in the back.

Bliss
Conscious
Communication

A Co-creation
by Happy and _____
You!

ISBN: 978-0692322697

Written with admiration in joyous celebration of all who dare to inspire, especially a supernova of *Bliss Conscious Communication*, you!

Over many years, oodles of friends have asked,
"Happy, why are you so dang happy?"
This book is the author's response.

To procure individual or bulk Bliss books at the best price:
www.BlissologyUniversity.com/Books
BlissForth@BlissologyUniversity.com
To be in touch with your co-author:
Happy@HappyOasis.com

Bliss U Books
Heaven On Earth
4395 Lake Forest Lane
Prescott, Arizona 86301
928.308.2146

Loka samasta sukino sahtay.
May the whole world be happy.
May the whole world live in harmonious bliss. ☺

This Is Not A Silly Book

Happiness is a serious career.

Sharing skillfully is more essential than ever.
Bliss Conscious Communication celebrates
fun new ways to joyfully prevent conflict
while enhancing communion of the heart.

This book deepens joy in relationships.
It saves marriages, friendships and even lives -
possibly including yours.

These feats inspire *Blissipline*
as Happy's song suggests:

Our happiness must be deep enough
Our lives must be honest enough
Our speech must be kind enough

For harmony with each other
Brings peace to this world.

Words are mighty,
magical and prophetic.

A Prophecy

Bliss consciously we shall speak
With every brilliant ray of our being.
When listening is deemed
Sacred once more,
Communication will return
To *communion*.

Aware that each word wields
The power of the universe,
Able to perceive that every utterance
Is etched as if in fire across the sky,
We will rediscover
That even one thought expressed,
Yes, even a single word
Changes the world forever.

—*Esoteric Teachings of yppaH sisaO*

Dedication

To You - This Bliss Book's Coauthoring Blissologist,
to the Loving Words You Courageously Share
and to the Enjoyment Everywhere of
Bliss Conscious Communication
Because Our Mouths
Are Meant to Be
Sanctuaries
☺

Your Dedication

☼_____
_____
_____
_____
_____
_____
_____
_____

Contents

How to Absorb Every Iota of Bliss from This Book

Bliss Conscious Communication beams with brilliant quotes, *your* quotes. On every page await opportunities to create uplifting responses that are uniquely yours. With Blissipline, we will author herein a treasure trove of rip-roaring questions and inspiring proclamations. Feel free to quote yourself!

    Does your *communication* foster *communion*? It is intended to. Communication and communion are rooted in the same word, *commune*, which originally meant "together become one." Thus, regardless of how many words we speak or how many we hear, only when we "together become one" does true communication occur.

    What is the most common gift we give throughout the day? Words may be our commonest gifts. With words, we color and sculpt our worlds. We are what we think, say, and do, so why verbally hobble when we can verbally boogaloo?

    While we are yet alive, may we thrive by making magic of everyday conversations. Let the alchemy begin.

Galaxies of Gratitude to You for Coauthoring this Book with me.

Esteemed coauthor, ☼_____, may you unleash the wilderness of your heart and mind with ease as you coauthor this uniquely blissful book conjuring up your playful insights, profound philosophies, conversationally daring delights, and uniquely ecstatic expressions.

    Feel free to let yourself be outlandishly creative and ebulliently experimental as you activate your inner blisszillionaire, muse, and sage. On most pages, you will see several sun symbols "☼" that invite opportunities to creatively express yourself.

What Exactly Are the Blissiplines?

Blissiplines are the blissful disciplines featured in this book. Each chapter offers a sequence of Blissiplines for you to play with. Twenty chapters clearly point the way to uplifting options revealing the natural flow in which we delve into conversations.

The first chapters focus on inspiring introductions. The middle chapters explore a comprehensive array of bliss tips including overcoming the most common obstacles that sometimes prevent blissful communications from happening as well as dozens of ways to inspire happiness in your self, a prerequisite for being a Blissologist.

After a refreshing approach to conflict prevention and resolution, the final chapters finish with fantastic ways to say farewell to your friends and family that leave everyone glowing.

At least one new Blissipline is featured on each page, with a total of several hundred optional Blissiplines for your experimentation throughout the playbook.

By coauthoring this interactive book, the reader becomes adept at the Blissiplines thereby becoming a budding Blissologist. Blissology University certifies Blissologists with Degrees of Bliss.

A Blissologist is one who habitually practices the Blissiplines within; thus, consequently enjoys living in peace, harmony and happiness with frequent bouts of bliss.

1
Blissful Beginnings

Consciously Entering into a State of Wonder

To begin, let's jump in by turning within to wonder. Please consider your relationship with communication.

In discussions, which topics especially delight you?

☼ _____

☼ _____

What is it that most entices you to listen?

☼ _____

☼ _____

What most frequently inspires you to speak and share?

☼ _____

☼ _____

Which ways of speaking and ways of relating tend to open your heart-mind?

☼ _____

☼ _____

Which reasons for communicating do you feel are among the most beneficial?

☼ _____

☼ _____

What is it about certain conversations that leave you feeling particularly satisfied?

☼ _____

☼ _____

Questioning Common Questions

According to a recent survey, these are the seven most frequently asked questions in the English language:

- *How are you?*
- *What's your name?*
- *What do you do?*
- *Where are you from?*
- *How old are you?*
- *What time is it?*
- *What do you want to do?*

Do the above questions inspire you? They certainly didn't inspire me. Upon realizing this, I began to wonder, why do we ask what we ask?

☼ _____

What is the impact of the most common questions that we ask?

☼ _____

Questions are important. Until a generation ago, approximately one-quarter of our conversations entailed asking questions and two-quarters answering those questions. Bliss Conscious questions can guide our conversations into the most delightful realms. Questions are worthy of scrutiny and exultation.

Before asking anything of anyone, what if we were to first quietly question our questions in order to evaluate the worth of the questions we are about to ask? What would these pre-question questions be? Here are a few possibilities:

- Does this question accentuate the positive?
- Could this question lead to something wonderful?
- What questions can I ask that honor our highest aspirations?

Before asking a question, with which questions could you question your questions?

☼ _____

☼ _____

In the Spirit of a Quest, Let Us Ask Regal Questions

Quest is the root of the word *question*. *Quest* means *"to seek, to search for; an adventurous expedition."* Questions were originally posed as quests for deeply discovering the mysterious beings before us. May we embrace the spirit of asking a question as if we are embarking upon a noble quest. Let's reinstate this royal tradition.

It is our questions, even more than our answers, that most influence the course our lives, thereby determining our destinies. ☺

Which three questions do you most frequently ask others, and why do you ask them? As you ponder and explore, your answers will likely change and in turn change you. Knowing this, feel free to use a pencil.

1. ☼ _____
2. ☼ _____
3. ☼ _____

Which feeling or response does each of these highly influential questions tend to generate in you and others?

1. ☼ _____
2. ☼ _____
3. ☼ _____

Feel free to erase and enhance your answers as you experiment and feel inspired.

The spirit of asking caring and courageous questions means embarking upon a perpetual open-hearted quest. ☺

Experimenting with a Nexus of New
Bliss Conscious Queries

Since the ho-hum commonality of asking, *"How are you?"* sometimes elicits less-than-fabulous responses, let's concoct our own bliss-dipped questions. Merry queries evoke delightful responses. Knowing this, we can create uplifting new alternatives, such as these:

- *What's the bliss?* • *What's your beautiful and amazing news?*
- *How are you celebrating the miracle of life today?*
- *What's your focus of enthusiasm?* • *What makes your heart sing?*
- *Which intriguing ideas are you exploring?*
- *What is especially delighting you today?*
- *What are your most daring dreams and how are you manifesting them?*
- *What is your joy of being (j.o.b.)?* • *What are you loving most about life?*
- *How is your spectrum of reality expanding?*
- *How do you do?* • *How are your flowers growing?*
- *Why are you feeling especially grateful?* • *What would you love to experience?*
- *What's the good and glorious news?* • *What's up, Buttercup?*
- *Would you care to share something uplifting?*
- *What or who is inspiring you these days?* • *What are you aspiring to now?*
- *Where is the focus of your great love these days?*
- *What's stirring in your heart?* • *What's awakening in your heart?*
- *What do you value most in these changing times?*
- *Would you care to share an uplifting quote, joke or song?*
- *Would you please gift me with a treasured poem or parable?*
- *What's sacred to you?* • *How do you honor & express what's sacred in your life?*
- *To what are you dedicated?* • *What is your highest purpose?*
- *Which virtues do you most admire in people, and why?*
- *What is your soul song?* • *Would you sing a song or may I sing you a song?*
- *Have you heard about the glorious news? (Share any landmark good news.)*
- *Would you venture to share an inspirational highlight of your autobiography?*
- *What are you doing to help heal the planet, yourself and our shared Life family?* Or,

✿ --

Creating Your Own Bliss-Rich, Brilliantine Questions

What could you ask to inspire joy in others? What do you enjoy being asked? What are you most interested in answering and listening to others say? Explore initial inspirational hints for creating your own bliss conscious questions by wandering within. Also, feel free to glean ideas from the previous page and gather ideas from the verbs below.

☼ _____

☼ _____

☼ _____

☼ _____

☼ _____

☼ _____

☼ _____

☼ _____

☼ _____

☼ _____

☼ _____

A Sampling of Blissful Verbs

Abide, admire, ascend, aspire, astound, celebrate, commune, concentrate, create, dance, delight, discover, enhance, empower, encourage, expand, explore, express, enrich, enthuse, free, heighten, honor, illuminate, imagine, infuse, include, intuit, liberate, love, nourish, ponder, pray, realize, serve, share, sing, stretch, unite, uplift, wonder . . . (There are oh so many more.)

Which verbs or words of movement move you most?

☼ _____   ☼ _____

☼ _____   ☼ _____

We evolve only as ecstatically as our language evolves. ☺

Myriad Responses for Blissful Beginnings

With so many outstanding alternatives, does the question *"How are you?"* inspire you? It could!

   "How are you?" provides a golden opportunity to decide and define how we feel and, if we are conscious and enthusiastic enough, to uplift the conversational tone by transmuting mediocre responses such as "Pretty good" and "Fine" into creative bursts of joy. Here are several options to play with while you concoct a multitude of gleeful beauties of your own. *"How are you?"*

[Experiment by possibly saying this first:] *Wow! What a wonderful question. Thank you for asking.*
[Then, experiment with a few of these:] *I'm . . .*

• *Content beyond measure, thank you. And you?* • *Everything is so divine.* • *Grateful to be in the presence of an angel like you.* • *Fabulous, thanks to you.* • *Jubilant.* • *In love with life.* • *Blessed to be with you.* • *Delighted to be in your exquisite company.* • *Is life good or really good?* • *Blissed to be in your beautiful presence.* • *Glad to be alive right here right now with you.* • *We are so incredibly lortunate (lucky and fortunate), true or true?* • *Magnificent, are we not?* • *Absolutely fabulous to be here with you.* • *Scintillating.* • *Divine.* • *Sublime.* • *Effulgent.* • *Splendid being alive today, is it not?* • *Feeling Kaleidoscopic.* • *Whistling.* • *Today is the happiest day of my life.* • *Truly blossoming.* • *A song is in my heart.* • *Life is a glorious adventure.* • *Supremely glorious, gorgeous.* • *This moment is legendary.* • *Blissing in, blissing out.* • *Over the moon.* • *Loamy.* • *Sprouting.* • *Panoramic.* • *Gleeful.* • *Feeling a little less than excellent.* • *Partly cloudy with a chance of sprinkles in the afternoon.* • *I'm sure that on some dimension I am feeling fabulous.* • *Healing.* • *On an eye-opening adventure.* • *Enjoying this precious moment with you.* • *Invigorated.* • *Serene.* • *Thriving.* • *Enchanted to be with you.* • *The adventure continues, yes?* • *In awe.* • *What a wonderful question!* • *Grateful that we are friends/family. I celebrate you!* • *Feeling optimistic, thank you for asking. And you? How are you?*

✿ _____ ✿ _____

✿ _____ ✿ _____

Glad Greetings, Telephonically Speaking

Have you ever answered the telephone by saying, *"Yes! Yes! Yes!"* This glad greeting guarantees a grin as do oodles of others. For generic joy, I sometimes answer the phone by saying, *"Hi, Beautiful!"* to whomever may be calling. Many a surprised person on the other end has told me that it made their day. It's so easy and simple, so why not?

Some people believe that it is best to refrain from answering the phone with "Hello" since "Hello" is acoustically comprised of hell and low, neither of which is highly inspiring. In contrast to "Hello," these simple phone-answering options do inspire:

- *Hi! How ARE YOU?* (asked soothingly slowly with genuine caring and without pausing)
- *Good Tidings, Celestial Terrestrial, _____. How are you celebrating the day?*
- *I'm delighted to be in your telephonic presence. Thank you for calling. How may I help you? Or. . .*

✿ _____

✿ _____

✿ _____

Happy are the wise.
— a perennial adage

2

Astounding Answers to the
Seven Most Common Questions

Where Are We From? The Rare and Flagrant Truth

Little inspires us so much as hearing and sharing the rare and flagrant truth. Speech that is liberated from predictable responses perks our ears and opens us to wondrous possibilities. However, it is essential to be sensitively aware that when someone asks a question, such as "Where are you from?" in many cases such a "question" is in actuality a demand rather than a question asked in the spirit of an earnest and open-minded quest. This is partly due to the fact that many modern societies define strict parameters as how to answer common questions, especially "Where are you from?"

It can be surprising to learn that the dictates of civilization require a prepackaged *political* answer to the question "Where are you from?" as demonstrated in this conversation where a beginning Blissologist did *not* succeed in adding joy to the person joining conversation, yet gives us much to ponder.

I'm from _____ (any city or country). Where are you from?
[Budding Blissologist:] *Would you like to know the truth or the politically correct answer?*
I'd like to hear the truth, of course.
Then, I'm from the ethereal field from which all life is manifest.
What did you say?
The truth is, I come from the ethereal field, the substratum of reality. So, you look familiar.
I mean, where are you *really* from?
Just like you, I'm from the cosmic creative force emanating from an indefinable intrinsic essence present in the ether, wind, water, fire, sun, sky, stars and earth that comprise us and continuously stream through us.
What I mean to ask is, where were you born?
Do you mean geographically where did my mother happen to be at the precise moment when my body temple vacated my mother's uterus hundreds of moons ago?
Yes, that's it, precisely.
Geographically, this body was birthed on a great plain at the lip of a vast swamp.
You're not going to tell me where you are from, are you?
Do you mean politically, as in which city or state? Where do we really come from? Where were we before we were conceived? Now that's intriguing! Yes, that's what I want to know! Cities, states, and countries are political entities. Why in heaven would you like to know that? We've just met. Would you really like to relegate our conversation to the realm of politics?

Your Marvelously Mysterious Origins

The aim of *Bliss Conscious Communication* is to delight and inspire everyone we encounter. This requires sensitivity and respectful spontaneity. The beginning Blissologist (in the previous conversation) might have better avoided building up any potential frustration in that particular inquirer with a shorter response such as:

- *"I come from the ethereal field. And, I was born in New York."* Or
- *"I come from a place of creativity, freedom and sunshine - California."* Or

☼ ---

Where Did You Say You're From? I Mean, Originally.

If our new friends are yet to understand that we are speaking from an expanded place of truth, if appropriate, feel free to ask them a mind-bursting question such as:

- *Where are you from? I mean, where were you prior to your conception?*
- *Where were you from before your parents were born?*
- *Originally, where are you from, as in, prior to the birth of Earth? Who were your ancestors & what were they up to millions and billions of years ago?*

This immediate sharing of our greater connection serves to immediately connect us at a spiritual level. It is humbling and heart-opening to realize together that there is great mystery inherent in the excellent question "Where are you from?" How little we know about our ancestors prior to the dawn of humanity.

Since the precise date of the origin of humanity remains a fantastic secret and subject for creative conjecture, one honest answer could be,

- *I honestly don't know where I'm from. What a marvelous question.* [You can temper and ground this philosophical vastness by sharing your place of residence] *I come from the stars, I abide in peace, and I live in Malawi.* Or . . .

☼ ---

Expansively Ecstatic Yet Politely Pragmatic Responses

Here are a few other examples for succinctly bridging heaven and earth worthy of your consideration when asked, *"Where are you from"?*

- Where am I from? How profound. Do you enjoy philosophy? My home is in Iceland.
- I come from a place of joy and freedom. I was born in the Himalayas of India.
- I hail from a proud and ancient lineage of sperms and eggs. And, I'm from Vancouver.
- My people come from The Spider Woman. I grew up on Hopiland near Arizona.
- It is said that we were born from the eggs of a butterfly. I share this ancient lineage with my nomadic ancestors from China. In this life, however, I was born in Thailand.
- It's so mysterious. Nobody truly knows. Isn't it marvelous? And, I'm from Brasil.
- Are we not all born of stars and darkness? I recognize you. I'm also Australian.
- I was born in China, and these days I'm a happy wanderer, or what Happy calls a "yesglad". Why be a "nomad" when one can be a" yesglad"?
- I hail from Alaska's rainforest, the largest remaining temperate rainforest on earth, My parents are of Tlingit descent yet it is said my great aunt lived with the bears.
- I'm from Africa. Anthropologists contend that we all originated in Africa... And, this time around, I was born in London though my parents are Russian.

Imagine the geography of your birth. How would you most romantically describe it (without mentioning man-made structures such as hospitals or cities)?

☼ _____

What is the myth of your origin? Where would your ancient, nature-living relations say that they came from?

☼ _____

When asked where are you from, does your response generate curiosity, wonder and joy? What are the most luminous truths of your origin? Where are you truly from?☼ _____

Where are you based?	⇨	*I'm body based. And you?*
Where is your home?	⇨	*My home is in my heart...And, I call _____ home.*
How can I get a hold of you?	⇨	*By opening your arms. And here's my phone #.*
Where are you living?	⇨	*I'm living, and I'm here. Therefore, I'm living here.*

How Old Are You (*Really*)?

Fortunately, no law requires us to reduce the expanse of our magnificent life journey to a mere number. It's now acceptable to decide whether to share our relative "age". We are the sum of far more than numerals. We are ever changing, majestic works of art, innovation, beauty and genius, fabulously ancient, yet ever new. A more important question to ask yourself before answering, "How old are you?" is, *"Which age would I like to be right now?"*

If you are older, saying, *"I am perpetually seventeen"* or *"Going on thirty-nine"* or *"Not a day over one hundred twenty-nine years young"* may be whimsical, numerical alternatives for number-thirsty listeners.

Hooray, Eternal Enigma you, for realizing the freedom in occasionally choosing to honor the mystery of your time-transcendent existence by playfully responding to the question *"How old are you?"* when your sensitive wisdom deems it appropriately respectful and expansively-inspiring to do so with your particular audience.

- *Thank you for asking. I'm magnificent for any age (wink). Would you agree?*
- *I'm old enough to know that there are myriad intriguing ways to answer your excellent question. And you?*
- *Older than the flowers and younger than the mountains.*
- *I'm average for my age. I appreciate your curiosity. And you? Are you average for your age?*
- *We are beginningless, endless, timeless, and therefore ageless. True or true?*
- *How old is the wind, which whispers our antiquity? How old are the elements that continuously swish and swirl though us?*
- *If it's true that we are comprised of about 70% water, then most of me is water. So, the question is, how old is the water that streams through us? Billion of years old? I'm looking pretty darn magnificent for several billion years old, wouldn't you agree? (Optional) Last week, I turned 50.*

How old are you? ✿ _____

We don't stop playing when we grow old; we grow old when we stop playing.
—Finis Mitchell

31

What Time Is It? Creating the Best of Times

The common question *"What time is it?"* offers frequent opportunities for us to express *exactly what we would like to experience at any given moment.* With a bit of blissful contemplation, answering this question can evoke bursts of laughter while respectfully letting your listener know what the actual time is too.

Do you have the time?
Yes I do, thank you, and plenty of it. Would you like a little of my time? It's high 5.

"What time is it?"
- *What a marvelous question! Thank you for asking...*
- *It's time for a song.* (Sing a line of an uplifting melody.) *And, it's almost 2.*
- *It's time for a hug.* (If appropriate, open your arms.) *And, it's just past noon.*
- *It's time for celebration.* (Do a little jig, high ten, or spin around.) *And it's 3:42.*

✿ _____

✿ _____

"What time is it?"
What a delightful question. I'm glad you asked...
- *It's time to gaze.* (Said to loved ones, this offers a moment to commune in silence.)
- *It's time to dance.* (If appropriate, ask, "Shall we?") ... *It's midnight.*
- *It's time for appreciation, and I appreciate you... It's almost dawn.*

✿ _____

✿ _____

Wherever we go,
it's essential to make good timing,
with the emphasis on good.
—Ken Pirsig

Your Destiny Is in This Word

Have you ever considered which one word has the most impact in our lives? The most important word in your life, the word of singular influence, is the birth mantra, commonly known as your given name. Wisdom keepers know that the frequencies, tones, and attributes of our names influence our destiny. What is the meaning of your decidedly important first name?

✿ _____

What were the original meanings of your middle and surname(s)? (If you don't know, please find out.)

✿ _____

How do these name's meanings, sounds, and associations show up in your life?

✿ _____

Do your first, middle and last names most powerfully express your highest truths? If so, how?

✿ _____

How did you or your parents choose your first name? What was your name's significance?

✿ _____

Do you enjoy your names' melody of sounds? Why or why not?

✿ _____

How do you feel in relationship to the name you use when you introduce yourself?

✿ _____

Due to a name's far-reaching significance, naming a child is traditionally a sacred rite, which often entails praying and fasting, climbing a mountain, possibly consulting an oracle, the stars, a grandparent, a spiritual leader, council of elders, astrologers, signs, and one's own dreams, all the while closely observing the child, whether born, or yet-to-be-born, with reverence.

Have you observed how the ancient meanings of names influence people's chosen life paths? What impact does your name have on you?

✿ _____

What's Your Name? *What's Your Favorite Word?*

Here's an easy means by which to offer everyone the rare, exquisite pleasure of uttering their favorite words.

> *"What's your name?"* he inquired.
> *"What's your favorite word?"* she asked.
> *"Splendiferous,"* he responded.
> *"Amazing,"* she declared. *"My name is Splendiferous."*

Which words do your closest loved ones especially cherish? (If you have never asked, you may be delightfully surprised.) Please jot them down to sweetly honor them in future conversations.

✿ _____ ✿ _____
✿ _____ ✿ _____

For added happiness, offer your loved ones the opportunity of calling you by their favorite words, and inquire as to which names they would most love to be called.

✿ _____

Not so long ago, naming was frequent, fluid, and fantastically fun. Today's naming rites are sometimes meaningless, diametrically opposed to the elaborate naming rituals of our ancestors or antiquity. In the past, when something significant arose in the course of people's lives, they would occasionally offer each other new names in commemoration.

In ancient times, people also renamed themselves when they stepped into life anew by embracing an expanded understanding, a fresh identity, a transformative experience, mastery of a skill, or a new calling. Consequently, most everyone enjoyed several names. Ancient people were sometimes addressed by as many names as the number of people they knew. What a wonderful way to remind us of our multi-faceted dimensionality. Feel free to embrace such ancient and empowering traditions in your uniquely special way or create your own.

✿ _____

Self-Entitlement Experiments

While traveling exuberantly one month, I decided to don a new name each morning. This is relatively easy to do when backpacking alone through the mountains, and thereby walking daily to a fresh location. I'd often arrive somewhere at twilight, thrilled to bed down on a patch of pebbles in a meadow beneath the stars. I decided that at each dawn, as the first morning rays revealed the new surroundings, I would spontaneously choose a new name for the day from the first thought that sprang to mind.

Surprisingly, several of these experimental, daylong names such as Miraculous, Glad-to-Be-With-You, Iluvu, Spontaneous, Audacious, Lightning Blossom, Absolutely, Free, Snow, Smiling Heart, Sunbeam, Photon, Proton, Blisston, Quiet, Quintessence, and Allelujah produced such fascinating experiences, elicited such intriguing responses, and felt so satisfying that by evening I would wish the day would endure forever! On some days, songlike names, succulent to the ears, of unknown origins, and never written, would be chosen such as Hiyatahay, Malamalah, and Zubaluwubalu.

Consistently calling oneself by a new name throughout the day is a powerful Blissipline that arouses profound shifts in consciousness. Names are incantations. While a carelessly chosen name can harm, a carefully chosen name can charm, heal, liberate, and empower a person. Savvy adventure anthropologists know that those tribes renowned for their unusual joyfulness respected the time-treasured tradition of carefully choosing only names rich with expansive meaning.

If you were to change your name, what would you choose to call yourself today? How about tomorrow? What do you deeply love? Which words embody your essence? What is important, true, and beautiful to you?

Reverently yet playfully may you give tribute to your highest self by choosing oodles of new names, while remembering that names are also self-fulfilling prophesies.

☼ _____ ☼ _____

Using splendid monikers are reminders that bliss is our birthright. ☺

Who Are You?

Who are we *really*, aside from our parentally given names? We are, of course, the authors of our own amazing lives, free to define ourselves as delightfully and daringly as we can imagine. *"Who are you"*? Feel free to ponder these responses.

- *Who am I? What a wonderful question. I am inspired to be in your company.*
- *I'm Heavenly and this is Butterfly, thank you for asking. And you?*
- *Thank you for asking. I am a celebration of life, and I celebrate you!*
- *I'm a brilliant, strong and beautiful, just like you. True or true?*
- *I am a Certified Blissologist with Blissology University.*
- *I am a mystery, and so are you. Luscious to embrace the mysterious, is it not?*
- *Who am I? A marvelous question. Bliss is my true nature. What's your true nature?*
- *We are universal superstars. Would you concur?*
- *I am a lifestyle godzillionaire and a happiness billionaire.*
- *I'm a child of the sun, glad to be in your radiant presence. Thank you and you?*

Instead of automatically answering *"Who are you?"* with the name your parents chose to name you, how would you greet the opportunity with your original creativity?

☼ _____

☼ _____

☼ _____

☼ _____

☼ _____

☼ _____

Refreshing approaches evoke playful responses. ☺

What Do You (Love) to Do?

You will likely be asked, *"What do you do?"* on hundreds of occasions in the course of a single lifetime. Thus, the question *"What do you do?"* offers hundreds of opportunities for uplifting conversations while inspiring everyone you encounter, including yourself.

When someone asks, *"What do you do?"* imagine, if you could do *anything*, what would *you* *love* to do now?

☼ _____

☼ _____

☼ _____

☼ _____

Which actions generate the most joy for you?

☼ _____

☼ _____

☼ _____

☼ _____

What do I do?

- I appreciate, celebrate, and co-create.
- I love to snorkel, boogie board and sing while doing yoga on the sand.

When asked, *"What do you do?"* I mentally translate this question *into* *"What do I (love to) do?"* And you? What do you (most love to) do?

☼ _____

☼ _____

☼ _____

When asked, *"What do you do?"* Blissologists translate the question into
"What do I love to do?" and then respond accordingly. ☺

The Gracious Would Say Would

According to unabridged dictionaries, the original root of the word *"want"* means *"lack and desperation"*. These ancient meanings are less than blissful. Oh, what to do?

Fortunately, it's easy to formulate uplifting alternatives to the seventh most commonly asked question in the English language, *"What do you want to do?"* by replacing it with, for example, *"What would you like to do?"* or *"What shall we do?"* Other exciting options include:

- *What would you like to co-create?*
- *How shall we celebrate this occasion?*
- *What would you most love to do now?*

☼ _____

In the following conversational situations, how would you transmute *"want"* into *"would"*, *"shall"*, *"like"*, *"love"* or something joyous else?

Do you want something to eat? (For example, Would you like . . .)

☼ _____

Do you want a glass of water?

☼ _____

Do you want to climb behind a waterfall and sing to some wild elephants?

☼ _____

Kindly create a question that you sometimes say that includes the word "want".

☼ _____

Then transform it.

☼ _____

Aim for the moon. If you miss, you just might hit a galaxy. ☺

Choice Opportunities

Have you ever felt so thoroughly *content beyond measure* from one marvelous moment to the next that life's mundane details sometimes seem relatively unimportant? If, when in such a blissful state, I'm asked, *"What would you like to do?"* I have made the mistake to carelessly say, *"I don't care."* However, saying, *"I don't care"* may be misleading since, of course, we certainly *do* care.

So that a carefree *"I don't care"* attitude is not misconstrued as apathy, we can rejoice in our carefree feelings by giving our loved ones those opportunities to decide. When asked, *"What would you like to do?"* instead of responding with, *"I don't care,"* how could we more joyously and generously respond?

- *I am feeling so carefree and content that I'd love it if you would choose.*
- *Your choice, Gorgeous. I'll be happy with whatever you decide.*
- *It would gladden my heart if you would take the lead.*
- *As you like, Precious. Surprise me!*

☼ --

Expressing Enthusiasm for Splendid Suggestions

How can we habitually encourage the sharing of creative ideas while overcoming any habitual resistance to suggestions? By agreeing enthusiastically. Even if you may privately entertain other perspectives, what would you say to respectfully and ebulliently express appreciation for others' ideas?

- *Insightful, thank you. Your idea is worthy of consideration.*
- *Wow!* • *What a marvelous idea.* • *Brilliant insight yours.* • *A fabulous hypothesis.* • *Let's!*

☼ --
☼ --

The more you celebrate life, the more there is in life to celebrate.
—Oprah Winfrey

The Importance of Being Zany

Fortunately, there is no need to ever be bored again for even a single second. With the slightest exertion of our muscle called *creative imagination*, a mind-boggling infinitude reveals itself, ready to be delightfully discovered at our beck and call.

Instead of habitually asking friends and family, *"What would you like to do?"* we can activate our creative imagination about unusual, tantalizing, resplendent and downright zany activities now to draw from later during occasional droughty moments ahead. How often do you surprise your loved ones? How did you last surprise them? And, most importantly, how would you like to surprise them next with some splendid adventure or simple gift?

✿ _____

If you ever feel stumped, feel free to take up any of the following activities enjoyed from my colorful past. That's what friends are for.

- *Let's snorkel in the dark. (or anytime any-beautiful-where we can)*
- *Let's secretly fill people's shoes with flowers.*
- *Let's sing out our conversations. • Let's dance our deepest meanings.*
- *Let's light a candle to enhance our evening.*
- *Let's agree to get chummy with the next insect we encounter.*
- *Let's write, tape up, and hand out uplifting haikus or flowers at bus stops.*
- *Let's crawl everywhere for the rest of afternoon.*
- *Let's secretly "love vibe" and openly compliment everyone we see.*
- *Let's dance and hum consciously in harmony and record it for posterity.*
- *Let's run barefoot on the beach. Let's let our feet feel the soft earth & grass.*

Which creative, unusual, pleasantly adventurous activities would you and yours enjoy? Let's . . .

✿ _____

✿ _____

✿ _____

Let's Explore More Possibilities

When there is a world to explore and celebrate right beneath your nose, why succumb to the boob tube, smart phone or computer for entertainment? What else can you imagine doing for pure delight, fun, adventure, relaxation, health, happiness or *_____?

- *Let's pray in new ways.* • *Let's spoon feed each other an entire meal.*
- *Let's create beautiful music together at every opportunity.*
- *Let's pin up poetry in public places that could use more cheer.*
- *Let's lead sing-a-longs beneath trees.*
- *Let's grow a garden and sprouts in jars.*
- *Let's innovate, write and sketch out new inventions by the light of the moon or candle.*
- *Let's silently picket in forlorn places to legalize happiness with smiley signs.*
- *Let's create a flamboyant dinner party smorgasbord where everything co-creative and intriguing but food and drink is served.*
- *Let's remember and reinvent ancient ways of being.*
- *Let's gently walk up to one stranger at a time and sing them a song.*
- *Let's write poemettes, sonnets and other giftlets to share inside our home.*
- *Let's hike and chant our way up a mountaintop by the glow of the full moon.*
- *Let's speak in various accents and act out different personalities for a hoot.*
- *Let's learn our favorite second language and speak it for fun together.*
- *Let's draw hints and paint glimpses of invisible worlds as gifts.*
- *Let's secretly, respectfully and playfully give donations to friends in need.*
- *Let's sleep al fresco on the roof, patio, lawn or beach beneath the stars.*
- *Let's foster a golden cause.* • *Let's adopt endangered animals and plants.*
- *Let's co-create heaven on earth.* • *Let's originate, explore and consecrate.*
- *Let's see how loving, free, wise, magnanimous and zany we can be.* ☺

Let's . . .

✿ _____

✿ _____

3
Inspiring Introductions

Exuberant Endearments

What if, suddenly, on the brink of asking a *Bliss Conscious* question, nothing inspiring springs to mind? Fortunately, there are abundant other untold introductory options. For instance, adding uplifting nicknames to the beginnings, bellies, or endings of greetings also kindles mirth.

Do faces brighten whenever you exclaim *"Good Morning, Sunbeam!"* with heartfelt enthusiasm? Concoctions of exuberant endearments are as infinite as the imagination. Co-authoring Blissologist, please let your inborn creative genius loose! For example, feel free to experiment with these:

- *Good Tidings, Extra Celestial Terrestrial.*
- *Hello, Treasure Trove.*
- *Greetings, Godus.*
- *Good Evening, Thunderbolt.*
- *Marvelous Moment, Exquisite Embodiment of Divine Perfection.*
- *Hi, Angel, what's the bliss?*

☼ _____

☼ _____

☼ _____

How can we honor friends, both new and old, in our midst?
- *Thank you for gracing us with your presence.*
- *Delighted to meet you.*
- *Sweet to see you again.*
- *Glad to be here with you.*
- *I'm honored.*
- *The pleasure is mine.*

☼ _____

May we frequently anoint one another
into a culture of ceaseless celebration. ☺

Co-Creating Beautiful People

Everyday conversations can be fairytales if one enjoys waltzing with words. Our blissful lips can paint luscious terms of endearment lavishly reminding everyone how special we all are and how wonderful we can be. Uplifting epithets pose friendly means for joyously addressing whomever we encounter. Let's declare our most playful perceptions of the precious human gifts before us.

By being pragmatically ecstatic and unabashedly friendly, we invite people to do the same. Appreciation is irresistible, especially when personalized. We can concoct cheery epithets for addressing our esteemed associates such as " Erica Ecstatica", "Joy Called Johnny" and "Miraculous Miltonious."

Spontaneously jot down the names of seven special people who feature most frequently and significantly in your life, then beget an endearing epithet for each. Rhyming and alliteration are optional.

1. ☼ _____
2. ☼ _____
3. ☼ _____
4. ☼ _____
5. ☼ _____
6. ☼ _____
7. ☼ _____

Each generous gesture generates a new generation of uplifted creation, thereby opening up new world of magnificent possibilities each day. ☺

*Let's legalize happiness
starting with our daily conversations.* ☺

Initial Blissful Courtesies

The origin of a smile is usually another smile.
– somebody

Amidst the bustle of modern city life, initial blissful courtesies are frequently forgotten. Fortunately, there is an easy antidote to moments of conversational alienation, a very simple way to restore friendliness and human dignity. It is this: before asking for anything from anyone, *be friendly first*—no matter how inwardly focused or rushed you may choose to be.

Creating pleasant moments of sharing and caring in every conversation heightens our life experience immeasurably, even when simply asking for directions, as illustrated here:

Glorious day, is it not? Exceptionally splendid morning to you! How are you on this marvelous Monday morning? (And if all is well) Glad to hear it. I'm feeling rather fabulous myself. Considering that I'm lost, would you be so generous to tell me the way to…? Thank you so much for making this world a better place to live. May you enjoy this day to the utmost.

When you ask for directions, for your bank balance, for your restaurant bill or grocery receipt, what could you say to add to someone's happiness?

✪ _____

✪ _____

✪ _____

Communication and communion come from commune
which means "together become one."
Communion is the core purpose
and essence of communication. ☺

Bestowing Encouragement for Empowering Dreams

With ease and grace (and a smile upon our face) we can foster our friends' dreams by bestowing morsels of encouragement. For example, to a friend who is convalescing, one could exclaim, *"Hi, Energy Temple of Supernatural Health!"* Or to an aspiring artist, *"Glad Tidings, Conduit of Creativity!"* Or to a budding musical performer, *"Good Morning, Marvelous Musician!"* Or to our beloved, *"Good Evening, Precious Pulsar of Perpetual Lovingkindness and Delight."*

What could you nickname your seven closest kith and kin specifically to empower them to pursue their dreams while thoroughly enjoying the rest of their lives to the fullest?

1. ✿ _____
2. ✿ _____
3. ✿ _____
4. ✿ _____
5. ✿ _____
6. ✿ _____
7. ✿ _____

Consider your most recent conversations outside of your circle of friends. How could you uplift other people you meet with uplifting epithets?

✿ _____

✿ _____

✿ _____

Experiment with complimenting your intimate relations,
even if it startles them at first.
Eventually expand the horizons of your heart
to beam the dreams of all. ☺

Spontaneous Introductions Spark Creative Conversations

Why do we address our friends with the same old dusty names day after livelong day, when creating intriguing novel names is such fabulous fun? For instance, imagine being at a party where you spontaneously decide to introduce two friends (whose names you have momentarily forgotten) in a new light. What would you call them? Feel free to gather fun words as they spontaneously spring to mind.

Here's an example of what I occasionally say upon realizing that I've temporarily mentally misplaced the names of two acquaintances from the past:

"It is my profound pleasure to introduce you two.
Butterfly, this is Heavenly. Heavenly, please meet Butterfly."

In most cases, after this introduction, "Heavenly" and "Butterfly" will be delighted, conversationally at ease, and smiling, if not giggling, since almost everyone enjoys an unusual term of endearment. With two friends, experiment with your own creative introductions.

When spontaneously introducing people to each other, the more ecstatic, poetic and beatific the names you use, the better. The more spectacularly fun and exuberantly majestic and in-the-moment our terms of endearment, the more broadly everyone will grin.

How might you spontaneously introduce people?

☼ _____

Diplomatic hint: Experiment by making introductions with flamboyant pomp and ceremony, as if you are introducing royalty (because you are). For example:

With exquisite delight, I introduce the legendary . . .
It's a great honor to introduce you two illustrious . . .
With a glad heart, I'd love to introduce you to a magnificent exemplary of...
I am glad to be in the luminous presence of two of the most remarkable people . . .

Outlandish introductory compliments can beget bliss conscious communication.

4

Do You Love Your Life?

Celebrating These Precious Days

How do you honor happiness in your every day life?

Daily we do oodles of activities from serving the world to stretching to brushing our teeth; from envisioning our life movie to concocting a green smoothie. Let's take an intimate look at these priorities. In the left column below, lovingly list the estimated times you spend doing your twenty most common activities, those that represent the great bulk of how you most love living your precious life.

   Begin with the activities to which you give the most time. The first will likely be either sleeping or your J.O.B., your Joy of Being. Please get specific. For example, you might include commuting, cleaning, conversing, corresponding, shopping, preparing meals, dining, washing dishes, showering, singing, talking on the phone, texting, planning and pondering, relaxing, napping, computer time, quality time with your beloved or best friend or child or pet or plants, and time for your most energizing specific physical exercises and cherished creative pursuits.

Hours/Minutes Daily   Name of Choice Activity

1. ✿_____   ✿_____

2. ✿_____   ✿_____

3. ✿_____   ✿_____

4. ✿_____   ✿_____

5. ✿_____   ✿_____

6. ✿_____   ✿_____

7. ✿_____   ✿_____

8. ✿_____   ✿_____

9. ✿_____   ✿_____

10. ✿_____   ✿_____

Total ✿_____ hours

• Please prepare to share the second half of your top activities on the next page.

What is my Joy of Being? Is my J.O.B. my Joy of Being?
Do the activities I do all day give me joy? If yes, hooray! If not, why not? ☺

We Choose *Everything* We Do

Some see things as they are and ask, "Why?"
I dream of things that are not, and ask, "Why not?"
—George Bernard Shaw

Have you ever wondered precisely where does the time go? If you are running out of ideas of how you spend your treasured time, feel free to delve a little further to rediscover many more deliciously detailed activities of your daily celebration of life.

	Hours/Minutes Daily	Name of Choice Activity
11.	☼ _____	☼ _____
12.	☼ _____	☼ _____
13.	☼ _____	☼ _____
14.	☼ _____	☼ _____
15.	☼ _____	☼ _____
16.	☼ _____	☼ _____
17.	☼ _____	☼ _____
18.	☼ _____	☼ _____
19.	☼ _____	☼ _____
20.	☼ _____	☼ _____

Total ☼ _____ hours (= 24 hours from both pages).

Did you include all twenty activities from both pages? Be sure that the time for all of the activities you've listed on both pages totals 24 hours. Thank you. Let's look lovingly at what you've written, at how you choose to live your days and nights.

Which portions express your most and least cherished values?
☼ _____

What does your life reveal about your life?
☼ _____

According to what is not on your activities list, what don't you value?
☼ _____

Your Ideal Lifestyle

Assuming your ideal lifestyle is already coming true, how would you like to divide the remainder of your precious days? What is a dreamy day for you? What would you enjoy doing and being more often and most of all?

✿ _____

✿ _____

✿ _____

What would you prefer to minimize or delete?

✿ _____

✿ _____

Which others would you like to maximize or add?

✿ _____

✿ _____

✿ _____

Returning to these twenty activities, feel free to make notes beside them to clarify how you would ideally like to most fully enjoy your treasured remaining days. Modify the hours accordingly so that they still total twenty-four.

Bliss-consciously designing your lifestyle in turn determines your destiny. ☺

Which choices could you make to narrow any disparities between your current lifestyle and your ever more luminous lifestyle?

✿ _____

✿ _____

Don't tell me what you believe. Tell me what you do
twenty four hours a day, and I'll tell you what you believe.
—Jerry Ruben

51

Defining Yourself

Words are mighty, magical and prophetic.
First accessing my infinite potential, I speak. ☺

However we define ourselves reveals who we are and portends who we will be.
How do you describe yourself both to others and to yourself?

✿ _____ ✿ _____

✿ _____ ✿ _____

How could you lovingly steer self-deprecations toward emphasizing what's
glorious in your conversations? For example, how can we respond if someone
says, *"I realize that I can't do this. I'm just not a skillful communicator."* How
about this: *"Do you mean that you are a blissful beginner determined to
communicate ever more consciously? I celebrate your honesty and applaud your
humility. You're amazing."*

✿ _____

Consider two aspects of yourself that you sometimes perceive to be less-than-
excellent? How could you creatively redefine these in a more playful, positive,
celebratory light?

✿ _____

✿ _____

Martin Luther King didn't say,
"I have a complaint,"
"I have a problem,"
or "I have a difficulty."
He said, "I have a dream."

Delightful Addictions

The word *"addiction"* is an etymological conglomeration of *diction* meaning *"speech"* and *ad* meaning *"to."* Hence, addictions are *"what we speak to"* people about, including ourselves. Our addictions are the foci of our enthusiasm. Thus, contrary to popular understanding, in this meaning, addictions may be not only beneficial, but also fantastic.

Religion originated from *re*, which meant *"again,"* and *legion*, which meant *"allegiance."* Thus, our *"religion"* is whatever we give *"allegiance to again."* The ancient root of *allegiance* is *"loyalty."* Our addictions (what we speak to people about) form our core religion (our allegiance or *"loyalty again"*).

To what thoughts and topics are you most loyal again and again? Which themes most frequently frequent your conversations? Which "subjects of your enthusiasm" do you most habitually "speak to"? In other words, which five topics comprise your primary conversational "addictions" while alone with yourself and also with others?

1. ✿ _____
2. ✿ _____
3. ✿ _____
4. ✿ _____
5. ✿ _____

If the above "addictions" represent five foundational tenets of your "religion", which facets of "your unique religion" do you value most and least, and why?

✿ _____
✿ _____
✿ _____

Considering what you most commonly speak to, would be an appropriate name for "your unique religion"?

✿ _____
✿ _____

Complimenting Complimenters

Do you usually receive compliments gladly, humbly, and graciously with exuberant appreciation? Please expound.

✿ _____

Are you generally a joy to compliment? Why or why not?

✿ _____

It's a blissful blast to deeply receive then radiantly reflect the kindness and generosity of gracious praise back to those who compliment us instead of quietly absorbing them. For instance, when someone offers encouraging words, we can boomerang praise back in a variety of playful ways.

For example if someone comments, "The way you speak is so delightful and inspiring," you might respond,

- *Thanks be to luminous you!*   • *How kind and generous of you.*
- *Your words reveal your beautiful heart.* • *How loving.*
- *What a thoughtful observation.*   • *I appreciate your encouragement, thank you.*
- *You are inspiring me to do my best to live up to your generous perceptions.*

✿ _____

We can enjoy affectionately complimenting critics, too. Thanking critics disarms us all, fosters peace, and preserves everyone's dignity. Whether we feel that the criticism rings true or not, we can feel grateful that it provides food for reflection and an opportunity to put yourself and *Bliss Conscious Communication* to the test.

Who knows? Criticism may give rise to introspection that may result in character amelioration, compassion, tender tears, brilliantine epiphanies, spontaneous singing, cascades of laughter, surprising bursts of euphoria, emotional liberation, consequent celebration, and momentous leaps of understanding such as:

✿ _____

*Heart-enriching gifts arise from earnestly attempting to practice the art of
receiving praise & blame, fortune & fame, and loss & gain
with equanimity, grace and ease.* ☺

The Universe Is (Still) Deaf to Negatives

This, like so many words of wisdom, is easy to forget. *"The universe is deaf to negatives"* implies that Cosmic Intelligence is unable to hear negative words, such as *not* and *never*. Therefore, when "I am not . . ." is uttered, the Universe hears "I am . . ."

Thus, describing oneself as *not, no,* or *never* unwisely focuses ones thoughts upon what one does not wish for. Instead of repeating what you would rather not wish to experience, I dare you to boldly state your aims by positively proclaiming only that which you would love to welcome into your life.

If it is true that on one level *"The universe abhors a void, and loves for each of us to fill it,"* we will likely eventually experience whatever we persistently and intensely focus upon. Consistently positive speech creates astoundingly positive circumstances. Which circumstances would you especially love to womanifest? Or manifest?

✿ _____

Which habit would you like to transcend and which replacement activity would you ideally prefer to fill the void?

I'd prefer to . . .

✿ _____

How would you positively transmute the phrases on the left to a similar one on the right?

I don't like . . .	⇨	*I enjoy . . . or I prefer . . . or*

✿ _____

Don't fall and hurt yourself.	⇨	*Kindly proceed with care.*

✿ _____

No worries. It's not a problem.	⇨	*It's pure pleasure.*

✿ _____

It's no trouble at all.	⇨	*It's a joy.*

✿ _____

I'll never forget this.	⇨	*I'll always remember this. And you.*

✿ _____

5
Everyday Gladitudes

The Bliss List

The Bliss List is an easy way to check in with our conversational-emotional state of being. It is helpful to look at any time we are feeling down, especially during a disagreement. Where are you on the Bliss List now?

The Blissless frequently:		Blissologists frequently:
Complain	⇨	Celebrate
Compete	⇨	Cooperate
Condemn	⇨	Compliment
Moan and whine	⇨	Hum and Sing
Habitually interrupt	⇨	Breathe and Listen
Elicit tearful frowns	⇨	Elicit Tears That Blossom Grins
Beget bickering	⇨	Create Peace
Protect only themselves	⇨	Protect All
Dwell in the past and future	⇨	Consciously Live Presently
Are scattered	⇨	Are Attentive
Take credit	⇨	Give Credit
Avoid responsibility	⇨	Take Responsibility
React	⇨	Respond
Gossip and slander	⇨	Speak Generously or Minimally
Emphasize I, me, and mine	⇨	Emphasize We, Us, and Ours
Boast	⇨	Praise, Praise, Praise
Rush	⇨	Slow
Know	⇨	Wonder
Attempt to limit	⇨	Liberate & Illuminate
Sadden	⇨	Gladden
Emphasize differences	⇨	Celebrate Commonalities
Divide	⇨	Unite
Hear without empathy	⇨	Listen Deeply to Understand
Aim to be right	⇨	Love to Learn and Be Loving
Fear, shun and limit	⇨	Embrace, Encourage and Empower

Experiments with Conversational Alchemy

The words *don't, won't, can't, haven't, hasn't, aren't,* and *isn't* are verbal depressants that enfeeble the life force and dissipate dreams. How would you positively transform them by more cheerfully expressing the common complaints featured on the left?

What's wrong?　　　　　⇨　What's happening?

☼ _____

Are you ill?　　　　　　⇨　How are you feeling?

☼ _____

I don't want to get sick.　⇨　I aim to be healthier than ever.

☼ _____

You're not listening.　　⇨　We can be excellent listeners.

☼ _____

Don't worry.　　　　　　⇨　Have faith.

☼ _____

Don't shout.　　　　　　⇨　Shall we whisper? It's so much sweeter. (smile)

☼ _____

I won't . . .　　　　　　⇨　I would rather . . .

☼ _____

I don't want to . . .　　⇨　Instead, I'd love to . . .

☼ _____

We can't . . .　　　　　⇨　Perhaps we could . . .

☼ _____

I hate* . . .　　　　　　⇨　In contrast, I appreciate and prefer . . .

☼ _____

Only love overcomes hate. This is the law, ancient and inexhaustible.
—Buddha, Honorary Blissologist

It's a beginner's Blissipline to wholeheartedly renounce this harmful word. ☺

Broadcast Wonderful Habits

Shortly after I started backpacking around the world for years as an adventure anthropologist at such a pace that often resulted in passing every few evenings in a new home, I decided decades ago, for purposes of superb health and happiness, to take up the practice of sleeping al fresco.

Wherever I would stay the night, upon arrival, I would inform the hosts of "my *peculiar habit* of sleeping outside." Consequently, dozens of accommodating friends, half-heartedly yet graciously, offered their back gardens, front lawns, porches, gazebos, children's tree houses, and verandas—as if I were a most peculiar person with a most peculiar habit.

One evening, upon approaching yet another friend's home, it dawned on me that instead of awkwardly explaining, "I have a peculiar habit," a Blissologist would instead confidently and enthusiastically announce with panache, "I have a *wonderful habit*: I always sleep al fresco".

From that moment forward, to my amazement, whenever I slumber al fresco, by the second cloudless night, the hostess and host eagerly request to join me in sleeping beneath the stars.

Upon returning to my *Heaven On Earth* retreat in a verdant labyrinth of canyons deep inside the gorgeous Granite Dells amidst the highland lakes of Arizona, this *wonderful habit* became so infectious that all of my house guests decided to sleep outside. Thus, the bedrooms were left empty at night while the decks were filled with contented stargazers. We eventually built more decks and roofless cliff dwellings to accommodate star struck retreat guests since we were all joyously rediscovering the romance of the great outdoors.

As this example shows, by modifying a single word, we can enhance the quality of innumerable lives, including our own. Which of your *preferred* habits, preferences, ideas, and particularities could you re-present as being a *splendid* habit, *fabulous* preference, *phenomenal* idea, or *marvelous* way of being?

☼_____☼_____

To inspire everyone to wonder, speak from a heart of inspiration and wonder. ☺

Yes! The Shortest & Most Powerful Mantra

When answering your phone, instead of saying, "Hello," have you ever tried exclaiming, *"Yes, yes, yes!"*? I invite you to try it at your next three phone-jingling opportunities. What happens? How do recipients respond on the other end?

☼ _____

Yes can heal and manifest miracles. *Yes* is an actualizing word. *Yes* is the shortest and most powerful mantra. To enjoy the many healthful benefits of hearing *Yes* often, consciously frame questions that encourage others to say *Yes* to you. It's a blithe Blissipline to refrain from asking queries that require "no" responses.

For example, "Do you mind if I . . . ?" is a *negative* question, because to answer it affirmatively requires saying, *"No,* I don't mind." It also assumes botheration in contrast to the freer, open-ended question, *"How would you feel if I . . . ?"* This simple and wonderful question offers an infinite spectrum of responsive opportunities.

Asking *"Are you okay?"* suggests that someone is either okay or less than okay. However, the recipient may be feeling far happier than the realm of ho-hum "okay" describes. The recipient may be feeling sublime, kaleidoscopic, or content beyond measure. Thus, my friend, consider refraining from asking, *"Are you okay?"* since it is a constrictive black-and-white question which requires a yes or no answer.

By simply asking, *"How are you?"*, in contrast, you open up a full spectrum rainbow of expressive options that may stimulate spontaneous, creative, authentic, openly honest, or boldly joyful responses. How would *you* blissify the questions on the left?

Do you mind if I . . . ?	⇨	*How would you feel if I . . . ?*

☼ _____

Would it bother you if I . . . ?	⇨	*If fine with you, I'd love to . . .*

☼ _____

Is it a problem if I . . . ?	⇨	*Would it be agreeable to you if I . . . ?*

☼ _____

Are you okay?	⇨	*How are you feeling?*

☼ _____

Admirable Virtues of Your Seven Treasures

Which seven treasured people feature most frequently in your life, and among these closest associates, which qualities do you admire most in each?

Names of Family and Friends	Their Virtues
1. ✿_____	✿_____
2. ✿_____	✿_____
3. ✿_____	✿_____
4. ✿_____	✿_____
5. ✿_____	✿_____
6. ✿_____	✿_____
7. ✿_____	✿_____

To witness loved ones blossom, focus attentively on their virtues. ☺

Which virtues do you most appreciate about yourself? (I dare you to fill these out.)

✿_____	✿_____
✿_____	✿_____
✿_____	✿_____
✿_____	✿_____
✿_____	✿_____
✿_____	✿_____
✿_____	✿_____
✿_____	✿_____
✿_____	✿_____
✿_____	✿_____
✿_____	✿_____
✿_____	✿_____

I am wonderful. I love myself unconditionally. I am precious. I adore me. Repeat.

6
Cultivating Inner Cheer

Blissing Forth Is Our True Nature

With wise and lucky life choices, the option to be happy and content most of the time, even enjoying the bliss of peace, is virtually omnipresent, since bliss is the undercurrent of creation. Bliss is our true nature whereas other states can be rather curious dramas. Whatsoever we expansively embrace, we most often become.

Are there any thoughts that you choose to think or emotions you chose to feel that delay you from living in almost continuous bliss while honoring the deep rainbow of emotions? If so, how could you cheerfully redefine these?

✿ _____

Deep meditation and observation reveal that *thoughts precede emotions*, if even by a fraction of a second. This is very good news, especially for Blissologists.

Moreover, nobody owns emotions. We simply pick them up. Feelings and emotions are not personal, but communal phenomena. Just like picking up a spoon from the communal bowl at the monastery where I lived in Thailand, we can just as easily pick up a feeling, hold on to it, and experience it. When we are finished with it, we wash it, then simply put the emotion back in the communal bowl as we do a spoon.

When we are conscious, we are free to pick up and put down feelings at our discretion. There is no such thing as "an angry man" or a "fearful woman." The anger does not belong to anyone. He is simply habitually clinging to a "spoon" of anger, while the she is gripping a "spoon" of fear, until they decide to put these down and pick up something else, if they are conscious enough. Consciousness and awareness are required to lead us to larger, more joyful perspectives and peaceful thoughts that result in harmony, homeostasis and happiness.

Every one of us has grabbed hold of the full gamut of emotions and will continue to do so. The question is: How do Blissologists clearly and quickly receive the wisdom-generating lessons to be able to most rapidly release feelings that have served their purpose? (The purpose of emotions is to let us know that something is awry.) When you find yourself in a state that is other-than-blissful, what do you do that successfully improves your mood?

✿ _____

✿ _____

Empowering Our Perceptions Expands Our Possibilities

What are your perceptions about life? How true, wise, uplifting, and fun are these basic beliefs? Freely complete these sentences by spontaneously sharing your most celebrated views of life, jotting down whatever inspirations spring to mind.

I . . . ✿ _____

Life . . . ✿ _____

The focus of my enthusiasm . . . ✿ _____

The human mind . . . ✿ _____

My mind . . . ✿ _____

The heart . . . ✿ _____

My heart . . . ✿ _____

The human body is . . . ✿ _____

My body is . . . ✿ _____

My creative offerings . . .   ✿ _____

My gifts . . . ✿ _____

The older I grow, the . . . ✿ _____

Relationships are . . . ✿ _____

My friends . . . ✿ _____

My most intimate relationship . . . ✿ _____

A home . . . ✿ _____

My home . . . ✿ _____

Traveling . . . ✿ _____

My loftiest dream . . .   ✿ _____

My greatest concern . . . ✿ _____

Nature . . I ✿ _____

Music . . . ✿ _____

Art . . . ✿ _____

Science and Computers . . . ✿ _____

Genius . . . ✿ _____

Communication . . . ✿ _____

I am most grateful for . . . ✿ _____

Delighting in Your Story Ignites Your Greatest Glory

Spirituality . . . ✿_____

The purpose of my life . . . ✿_____

My lifestyle . . . ✿_____

Humanity . . . ✿_____

Earth . . . ✿_____

The universe . . . ✿_____

Being alive . . . ✿_____

Freedom . . . ✿_____

Health . . . ✿_____

Success . . . ✿_____

Peace . . . ✿_____

Beauty . . . ✿_____

Wealth . . . ✿_____

Harmony . . . ✿_____

Love . . . ✿_____

My creative expression . . . ✿_____

My greatest asset . . . ✿_____

My highest spiritual truth . . . ✿_____

My vision or mission . . . ✿_____

This moment . . . ✿_____

My life . . . ✿_____

My deepest wish . . . ✿_____

The future . . . ✿_____

My most treasured idea . . . ✿_____

Which of the above views especially reflect your highest truths, catalyze the manifestation of your most delightful dreams, and enhance the lives of listeners?

✿_____

Words are meant to be soothing balms and cheerful miracles for the heart, especially in difficult moments. If any of the above perceptions could be expressed more joyously, feel free to play with them until merely reading them inspires you. Courageous coauthor, may this book be a ready friend and a tremendous source of inspiration for you and yours.

From Gloomy Doom to Blissful Bloom

When the shadowy bubbles of life arise, Blissologists avert temptations to overstate the negative by lovingly refraining from claiming gloomy truisms about the entire world. For example, broad pronouncements such as "You can't win," "Life is suffering," "Rain sucks," and "People are thieves" and "Technology is hell" amplify individual incidents, thereby needlessly projecting an exaggerated sense of hopelessness.

May you enjoy transmuting these gloomy pronouncements of doom into wild celebrations that bloom.

You can't win.　　　　　　⇨　　*The adventure continues.*

✿ _____

Life is suffering.　　　　　　⇨　　*Life is so precious, brimming with gifts.*

✿ _____

Rain sucks.　　　　　　⇨　　*Rain is beautiful. Rain is life. I love rain.*

✿ _____

Technology is hell.　　　　　　⇨　　*Technology is miraculous. I call upon the spirit of this delightful device to reveal how to proceed. I appeal to my ever-present genius to clarify this situation.*

✿ _____

Practicing techniques and implementing strategies that inspire you is paramount in order to enjoy equanimity while embracing upbeat options during challenging moments. ☺

Blissologists keenly observe everything, yet make little verbal note of inconveniences while making verbal mountains out of every iota of good. ☺

Empathetic Joy

Realizing the truth that *we are all related and entirely one* opens our hearts to the vastness of our being in a way that can seem at first almost too much to bear, blissfully so. Of course, this means that your joy is my joy, and my joy is yours. This includes our family of humanity and also our extensive families of plants, animals, minerals, and beyond.

"This is obvious," you-who-are-me may be thinking while reading this, which was written, of course, by you over here. When we experientially realize our essential unity, then envy and jealousy effortlessly fade away. Instead, empathy naturally arises, thereby opening the possibility for us to feel tremendous joy in another's joy, a quantum leap in expanding our bliss field.

Uttering "I feel jealous" or "I envy you," even in habitual jest, rapidly dilapidates a conversation. What can be said to transmute our own momentary feelings of envy into empathetic joy?

I envy you.   ⇨   *How marvelous. Your happiness is my happiness.*
✿ _____

I'm jealous.   ⇨   *Congratulations. Let's celebrate.*
✿ _____

If someone says, "I'm so jealous of you," how can we joyously answer?
More precisely, I think you are saying that you're happy for me. Thank you. I'm happy for you too.
✿ _____

Thank You Notes

If someone says, "Thank you", rather than responding, "You're welcome", it's sweeter to say, *"It's my pleasure. Thank you for the opportunity."* Outside of North America, answering "Thank you" with "You're welcome" implies unwanted obligation. Thus, in most languages the polite answer to "Thank you" is "It's nothing". In the USA, "It's nothing" is not considered to be a friendly expression, though in Australia saying, "No worries" replaces "You're welcome".

Uplifting Wisdom in Moments of Woe

The greater our compassionate lovingkindness, the more encouraging will be our speech. This is particularly evident in moments of woe and despondency. How to most soothingly respond when some dear heart, feeling crestfallen, is in our midst? When a forlorn friend glumly mumbles, "I can't bear to go on," what verbal gifts can we offer?

Perhaps...

- *Sweet, beautiful, precious being! Isn't it wonderful that all situations are impermanent?*
- *I am with you in the fullness of your sorrow.*
- *I deeply treasure your friendship. I love you. I am here for you.*
- *My love, shall we explore some positive possibilities, o super luminous sunbeam you?*

☼ _____

☼ _____

☼ _____

An Attitude of Gladitude

I continuously give thanks for the abundant gifts that life ceaselessly affords. ☺

Stating what we appreciate ecstatically expands our capacity to give and receive. By embracing the Blissipline of focusing on the marvels of this moment and proclaiming uplifting visions for ourselves and especially others, friends and family grin upon greeting us in glad expectation of our overwhelming gladitude.

What are a few of the *myriad blissings* that you, and possibly those with you, are grateful to be experiencing in this very amazing (when you deeply think about it) moment?

☼ _____

☼ _____

This bliss list is infinite when we fully present the present with our presence. ☺

Pity Weakens Whereas Compassion Empowers

What specifically distinguishes pity from compassion? While pity weakens, compassion empowers. Pity suggests, "I'm *sorry*. That is *dreadful* what happened to you." Consequently, the listener feels even more *sorry* and *full of dread*. Compassion, in contrast, calmly affirms, *"Let's look for the good in this situation. Tap your infinite strength, my friend. This could be a great opportunity in the making."*

What could you do, say and write that would empower friends and family to meet their current challenges with less pain and ever more confident, joyful hearts?

☼ _____

What could you do, write and say to encourage your self today?

☼ _____

The purpose of life is to experience happiness.
In order to achieve this, much depends on our mental attitude.
—Dalai Lama, Blissologist

Foregoing Futile Elaborations

Advanced Blissologists refrain from habitually saying, "In my opinion," "I think," and "I believe" prior to speaking since it is usually self-evident that any words coming from the speaker's lips express the speaker's perspective. These futile filler phrases needlessly dilute and slow the flow of ideas by subtly drawing the focus away from stimulating topics of shared discussion so that the speaker can enjoy more attention. This is merely my opinion. Hee hee.

May we . . .

☼ _____

May we constantly create potent verbal imagery that enables evolution. ☺

7
Joyous Solutions for
Conflict Prevention & Resolution

Transmuting Complaints into Relishing Requests

By emphasizing what we love and proclaiming it, accentuating the positive and exclaiming it, we can smoothly transmute our own complaints into relishing requests.

Commencing requests with "I love it when . . ." cheerfully emphasizes the inspiring side of whatever you would like to request of your loved ones, including your adorable self. Note, for example, the following *fundamental* forward shift in perception between these two:

I'd rather that you not . .   ⇨   I *love* it when you (we) . . .

What would you like to lovingly request more frequently in your life?
I love it when . . .
✿ _____
I love it when . . .
✿ _____
I love it when . . .
✿ _____

Overcome Inferior Feelings By Stating What You Love

Those of us who entertain thoughts of low conversational self-esteem can alleviate this by speaking up and stating what we'd love, instead of giving away personal power by asking excessive permission from other adults. The examples on the left needlessly disempower the speaker and trivialize the conversation, while those on the right empower healthful confidence and respectful equality.

Can I say something?   ⇨   *There is something important I'd like to add.*
Can I go to the restroom before you speak?   ⇨   *I'd love to give you my full attention. One moment please.*

Feeling free and happy is humanity's most underrated duty and delight. ☺

Pro-Creative Compliments

When something less-than-exceptionally superb transpires, we can offer alternative approaches that call upon our best, such as:
You are brilliantine, and I expect the best from you.

✿ _____

When something unkind is said, we can encourage virtues.
I love you for your genuinely gentle, kind, and considerate nature. I especially love listening when you speak from your highest wisdom, joy, humor, and compassion.

✿ _____

When someone poses limitations, we can suggest broader options.
Possibilities galore abound. This opportune situation is ripe with options. Together may we creatively call all excellent options forth.

✿ _____

*Let's live in joy
In love
Even among those who hate.
Let's live in joy
In health
Even among the ill.
Let's live in joy
In peace
Even amidst the upset.
Let's live in joy
In freedom
Shining radiantly
Wherever we may be.*
—Buddha, Honorary Blissologist

Verbally Expecting the Best in Others

We can create continuously blissful circumstances by envisioning marvelous outcomes. A fine way to predict the future is to create it by brilliantly entertaining and carefully sharing our most inspired visions and positive projections. How would you state what you would like to create in the following potentially challenging situations?

I don't' think you are going to cooperate.
Thank you in advance for your assistance.

✿ --

Looks as if we won't be able to agree.
I feel confident that we will reach an agreement.

✿ --

I think you intend to selfishly consider only your own interests.
Generosity is our true nature, and we both have generous spirits.

✿ --

You seem bent on destruction.
You are important and contribute to the world in a wonderful ways.

✿ --

About which facet of your future are you most enthusiastically concerned? What could you affirm to cast a positively inspired spell upon it?

✿ --

Is your glass of water that you share half empty or half full?
Is it half full of hope and joy, half full of sweet serenity?
Or is it full of water and air, abrim with kindness, cheer, and care? ☺

Feeling Fortunate & Free of Complaints

Associating with exceptionally fortunate people—those whose lives flow unusually smoothly and harmonically—can be intriguing. Deeply and persistently fortunate people exude a particular magnetic charm, demonstrating how habitual good fortune is often created with focused, uplifting actions, words and thoughts, including the heavenly habit of *amplifying gratitude*.

The interior activities of loving and wondering, laughing and relaxing, communing with one's highest source and visualizing the best possible outcomes for each scene in our theater of life, serve to accentuate and augment good fortune. Good luck is habit-forming, relative, and open to interpretation, as is its opposite.

Happiness is here for everyone. Perhaps surprisingly,
however, not everyone is here for happiness. ☺

It is a curious fact that some people are not truly happy unless they are perfectly miserable. And you? Do you entertain any cherished complaints, monstrous memories, frightening worries or fanciful woes upon which you occasionally or habitually dwell?

✿ _____

If so, what are the outcomes of vociferating these?

✿ _____

I once met two whining, "old" people in their thirties, whose miserable lives mirrored their mantra: "Life is nothing but a perpetual series of problems." Fortunately, everything is as awful or as *awe full* as we declare it to be.

How can we transmute "problems" into *creativity-enhancing gifts*? Could such opportunities be adventures, challenges, or light-paths to new possibilities? How else could "problems" be more luminously portrayed?

✿ _____

Would you like to free yourself of complaints? Is this possible? Absolutely! Complaining is habitual. Being free of complaints is easy with these two steps:

1. Stop complaining. 2. Start appreciating. ☺

On Being Problem Free

It's important to keep in mind that saying, "It's a problem" creates more "problems" by giving power to *problem consciousness.* Claiming to possess a "problem" compounds negative aspects of a scenario by needlessly arousing emotions associated with negative beliefs. In contrast, by interpreting experiences positively, we magnetize situational bliss and success. If someone says, "I have a problem," one uplifting, honest response could be:

Isn't it wonderful that it is our choice to perceive this situation as a problem, an adventure, or a creative challenge? Could there be more empowering ways to interpret this? Could it be a mysterious blessing or an opportunity to dive deeply, thereby expanding our capacity?

How might you respond?
- _____
- _____

Challenging situations may also be

inherently:	Or (feel free to unleash your creativity!):
Curious	- _____
Illuminating	- _____
Hilarious	- _____
Awesome	- _____
Balderdash	- _____
Mind-expanding	- _____
Educative	- _____
Preposterous	- _____

If I am for myself alone, what am I?
If not me, who? If not now, when?
—The Talmud

Breaking Through Your Bliss Bubble

One of the consequences of being a *Certified Blissologist* is discovering yourself to be frequently in the fine company of more gracious, glad, fascinating, happening, and fabulous friends than you had previously imagined possible. Why? You have grown joyful, fascinating, and wise enough to become a delightful magnet who attracts and nurtures the finest. You have honed your blissful skills to such an extent that you evoke hidden virtues in others. Congratulations.

At the same time, it's essential to understand that communicating with old friends and family may feel temporarily more challenging. Why? While you are internally and invisibly transforming, they may continue speaking the same way with you that they have for years. The biggest Blissipline is this: to love all our relations exactly the way they are—with affectionate caring yet unattached diplomacy, equanimity, compassion, humor, and unconditional celebration; meanwhile, harmoniously accepting that as we evolve, some may doors quietly close so that wondrous others may open.

How would you reframe the following?

Your way of communicating isn't blissful.
I love it when you conversationally inspire me with your brilliance and effervescent zest for life.

✿ _____

Why do you have to say that in such a negative way?
Shall we try this in an even more positive light?

✿ _____

I can't stand being around negative people.
I love being in the company of conscious and inspiring friends. Thank you for (often) inspiring me.

✿ _____

76

Reclaiming Reframing Opportunities

Occasionally, a person's unpalatable phraseology provides opportunities for you to quietly practice being a Blissologist with fiercely conscientious inner Blissipline. Consider that generally the denser the communication surrounding us, the less the potential for people's growth, exceptions excluded. In such circumstances, it may be wiser to calmly focus more on communicating politely rather than frankly, and on exuding peaceful understanding rather than trying to be understood, completely foregoing any frustrated fantasies of transforming the behavior of those around us.

For example, asking someone to speak bliss consciously may feel irksome thus unreasonable to the recipient. How can we bliss consciously inspire an interest, and thereby spark the slightest shift in consciousness by our own subtly sensitive, respectful, love-expanding example? Instead of requesting that associates reframe negative phraseologies, what are some polite, uplifting alternatives?

Occasionally asking, *"Could I reframe that please?"* gives us additional opportunities to hone our ever-budding talent for reframing. Sensitively checking in with others' moods and receptivity toward Bliss Conscious Communication is essential for success.

In many cases, with those unfamiliar with Blissology, it may be more helpful to simply reframe our sentences and occasionally reframe others', or, if need be, to kindly and very politely step out of the conversation. For instance, when someone says, "I hate prickly pears," you might offer, *"I understand that you are less than fond of prickly pears. May I enquire as to what you prefer?"*

To gently include others in a co-creative air, Blissologists have been heard wondering aloud, *"Hmm . . . interesting. Wondering how could we reframe that? Please understand, I'm participating in a course in Bliss Conscious Communication and our homework is to reframe any sentence we hear that might be addressed even more blissfully. May I try?"*

Most everyone delights in hearing their phraseology stated positively and exuberantly, though few are initially inclined to reframe their ideas themselves.

Which other gentle approach could you use to introduce joy-inducing reframing?
✿ _____

Could You Be an Occasional Conversational Terrorist?

Entertaining likes and dislikes is part of the human experience. It's how *lovingly* we describe our dislikes that influences the quality of our lives. Casually stating that something is "terrible" or "horrible" adds terror and horror to the world. Why be even an occasional *conversational terrorist?*

Impulsively blurting out negative statements, such as "I hate . . ." needlessly broadcasts hatred, fear, depression, irritation, frustration, constipation, and other despairing modes of dis-ease. Instead, we can softly state, "I prefer . . ." or vent with optimistic, life-enhancing expletives such as "Good heavens!" or:

✿ _____

✿ _____

If some less-than-excellent situation is commonly known, do you exercise the fortitude to refrain from claiming it to be awful, terrible, horrible, despicable, loathsome, dreadful, tragic, pitiful, shocking, yucky, abhorrent, abominable, odious, or unbelievably bad?

Sometimes, even friends and family unconsciously complain as an unskillful way of expressing caring. (For example, "What happened to you is terrible. That is awful.") In contrast, if caring is the consideration, let us say so consciously and positively. ("I care about you so much. How can we together deeply feel, then heal this situation?") Caring can also be emitted in silence by reaching out a hand while praying up wise and encouraging messages to share. What are some heartening alternatives for "That's terrible"?

Shall we take a moment to infuse everyone in this situation with love?
From a larger perspective perhaps this may be perceived as . . .
Strange as it seems now, some hidden blessing will soon grow out of this.

✿ _____

When you speak, your mind is on parade.
—Sai Baba

Unconditionally Wonderful People

At our health retreat in New Zealand, an unhealthy visitor grabbed my arm, then whispered, "I'm a miserable person and you should have nothing to do with me."

"You're a wonderful person," I retorted, fully meaning it.

"Aren't you quick to make a judgment!" snapped the visitor. "You don't even know me. Don't give me that crap."

As the hostess, I responded, "What you think and say about me and what you think and say about you will not change my opinion. I've already made up my mind. You are a wonderful person! I like you. It's that simple, and there's nothing you can do about it."

A few days later the visitor said, "Happy, you're my only friend here, and I'd like to give you something."

"You just did," I said as her hostess, beaming a smile with arms wide open, fully meaning it.

The Funny Factor Adds Mirth to Potentially Miserable Moments

• *Funny isn't it? Here we are in the rain without umbrellas! Without raincoats! Yet endowed with singing voices that could make the thunder listen.*
• *Funny isn't it? Of all the places in the galaxy to rendezvous, here we are standing in the same long line at a bank. What a fortuitous opportunity to enjoy your presence.*

In which situations could a splash of gladness brighten the moment?
Funny isn't it? . . . .

☼ _____

☼ _____

Saying we are sorry doesn't make us wrong and others right.
It means that we value our relationships more than our egos. ☺

When we listen very carefully, beneath it all, we can hear the whole world giggling.
☺
79

Easily Transmute Criticisms into Compliments

Do you occasionally encounter folks who tend to interpret compliments as criticisms? I decided long ago to interpret all criticisms as compliments, then to joyously return them to their owner. This delightful habit is astoundingly fun and freeing. It also brings potentially-lurking arguments to a swift, giggling halt.

What could be said if, for instance, someone calls you a rattlesnake? It only happened to me once, and I enjoyed it immeasurably.

"Thank you! I love rattlesnakes! Rattlesnakes can be gentle, frolicsome dancers, and highly telepathic. You are also rattlesnake-esque, as in smooth, grounded, and gorgeous, and that is the highest compliment! We have so much in common."

Imagine how someone could attempt to criticize you. How could you creatively interpret it as a compliment, then gleefully return it to the owner?

☼ _____

☼ _____

Remarkably Good Nights

Wishing someone "Good Night" assists in providing that person with a good night's rest. In this light, which words could convey the most optimum slumber?

For example, May consciously creative, wise, inspired, peaceful, restful sleep be yours. May you rest well amidst angels.

☼ _____

☼ _____

☼ _____

Looking up, we see the dark universe for what it is—an infinitude of chocolate love with bliss-dipped stars comprised of conscious coconut swirls. Feel free to concoct your own fantastic cosmic creation story here. God night. ☺

The "L" Word is The Cosmic Generator of Joy & Conversational Magic

Though curiously forbidden by some and overlooked by others, the "L" word is the substratum of existence and ironically also what this world needs most. But, what exactly *is* Love?

A man said to his psychiatrist, "I think I am in love with my umbrella."

"Hmmm," responded the psychiatrist. "Why do you think you are in love with your umbrella?"

"Because I *respect and appreciate* my umbrella *and very much enjoy being in it's company.*"

"Then," said the psychiatrist, "it appears that you are indeed in love with your umbrella."

By defining love, we may cozy up closer to it. If not the above psychiatrist's definition as respect, appreciation, and enjoyment, how would you define love?

✿ _____

I once lived at a monastery where the only time we were encouraged to say "I" was preceding the word "love" as in "I love . . ." Gladly exclaiming what we love with enthusiastic fervor delights and ignites hearts and dreams. Watch how conversations take flight when you simply voice a few facets of what you love about life, such as:

I love . . . ✿ _____   I love . . . ✿ _____
I love . . . ✿ _____   I love . . . ✿ _____
I love . . . ✿ _____   I love . . . ✿ _____

Which love stories, love songs, and love quotes do you especially love to share?

✿ _____
✿ _____
✿ _____

Lovely Mathematics: Universal Formulae
for Realizing Unity

Lovely Mathematics is unique in that the answer to every equation is already answered. Lovely Mathematics has cracked the riddle of the universe. While other mathematics focus on finding the solution to suit the equations, Lovely Mathematics aims to find equations to suit the solution. Since the solution has already been found, the rest is play, and this is precisely how the universe works.

Assuming the universal nature of the universe how can love be playfully expressed in equations?

1) 1 lovely us/she x he = oodles of us = 1 we = 1 lovely
2) 1 lovely gazing you + 1 lovely grinning me + 1 lovely we = we/me = we = 1 lovely
3) lovely us (you + me + she + he + they + we)/me = we = 1 lovely
4) If 7,000,000 humans = 1 humanity = 1 lovely

   and 23 billion know species = loveliness

   then, earthlings = 1 lovely x loveliness = 1 lovely

Even for those once erringly considered to be not-so-mathematically inclined, exquisite equations are now being discovered that are shedding new light on old love conundrums. How would you express your relationships mathematically? Geometrically? Algebraically? Quantumly?

✿ _____

✿ _____

✿ _____

We are wise to develop admiration and appreciation for one another.
—The Dalai Lama, Honorary Blissologist

Whatever you appreciate, appreciates.
—Marci Shimoff, *Happy For No Reason*

I-Free Conversations

A little less me, a little more we, elicits a sensation of unity. ☺

The words *I, me, my,* and *mine* are the treasures and the trappings of our precious egos. Though English speakers are usually unaware of this due to the pervasive use of the word "I", the more *I, me, my* and *mine* are said, the more we feel separated and alone. When during a conversation someone says *I, me, my* or *mine* prolifically, it creates a perception that the speaker is self-absorbed and not interested in the listener.

Do you ever wonder why you occasionally walk away from an otherwise perfectly fine conversation feeling unheard, unseen and unappreciated? A very subtle unspoken rainbow of associated emotions may be felt by the listener, emotions arising from the feelings of isolation, invisibility and exclusion. Saying "I" at the beginning of each sentence is considered normal in English, so sadness is imbedded in the language.

Consciously minimizing the use of the word "I" enhances joy, oratory intelligence and intimacy of the heart. Succeeding at being generally "I"-free is fun, challenging, considerate and conversationally commendable. *We* can easily do this by using *we, us* and *our* more frequently.

Feel free to experiment with speaking I-free for the duration of the next conversation, and please share your unusual results. If you are alone, consider picking up the phone to begin a telephonic I-free conversation with a friend.

What subtle shifts do you observe?

☼ --

Almost anyone can rekindle arcane ways of transmuting the competitive (exclusive) pronouns *I, me, my, you, they,* and *them* into the cooperative (inclusive) pronouns *we, us, one* and *ours.* Initially, this calls forth considerable Blissipline. Why can the pervasive American customs of commencing sentences with "I" be so challenging to relinquish?

☼ --

The Island Called We-land

forsake that place called me-land
of I, my, mine, and sorrow
alight on the i-land of we-land
of us and we and our.
wander the lands of love lexicon
inclusive affectionate fun
where never is heard a separatist word
where speech reigns inclusive, yes, one
☺

Moving from Me to We

ME and WE are mirror images. ME is WE upside down. ☺

<u>WE</u>

ME

You see, ME is topsy-turvy, which is rather uncomfortable. While saying ME depresses and distances, saying WE uplifts and unites. How would you transmute these common ME phrases into WE phrases?

I know.   ⇨   *That's true. OR We concur.*

☼ _____

I'm hungry.   ⇨   *Shall we enjoy some sustenance?*

☼ _____

I have an idea.   ⇨   *Let's…*

☼ _____

When we first speak I-freely for a while, suddenly we see the world differently. We may spontaneously speak less, listen more attentively, consider more deeply, and understand more holistically. Which kinds of themes and messages tend to be dropped in I-free, we-rich conversations?

☼ _____

☼ _____

☼ _____

Which kinds of themes and messages tend to flourish?

☼ _____

☼ _____

☼ _____

Dashing from Dislikes to Delights

Brilliantine Blissologist, would you be so kind as to momentarily consider two aspects of life about which you are less-than-enthusiastically fond?

1. ✿ _____

2. ✿ _____

Which feelings do each of these thoughts elicit?

1. ✿ _____

2. ✿ _____

Keeping these in mind, would you please share what you would prefer, enjoy, relish, cherish, admire, celebrate, or love in relation with these? Emphasizing preferences shifts the focus from litanies of dislikes to inspirational delights.

1. ✿ _____

2. ✿ _____

How do you *feel* when imagining each of these preferences?

1. ✿ _____

2. ✿ _____

Whatsoever we earnestly seek, we usually find.
Let's love ourselves enough to wisely seek out the beauty
of life with kindness of heart. ☺

Parable of the Ultimate Truth

Once upon a time, an avid seeker wandered the world in search of the ultimate truth. After countless years of arduous travel, the seeker learned of a highly respected sage who was reputed to know the ultimate truth.

The seeker set out to find her. Hearing that the wise hermit dwelt atop a particular jagged crag, the seeker trudged up and down vast rocky ranges, then finally up the said crag, thereupon encountering a fierce tempest of the most trying kinds.

Alas, after suffering great tribulation, the seeker reached the sage. Gasping for want of oxygen, the seeker implored, "Venerable One, what pray tell is the ultimate truth?"

"The ultimate truth is simple," giggled the sage gently, "is this: *Never argue with anyone.*"

"What?!" scowled the seeker, in bitter disappointment, feeling desperate for a worthwhile answer. "I haven't come all this way only to hear THAT. That's not the ultimate truth!" he shouted enraged.

The wise one paused to smile. "You may be right," she agreed meekly, wisely preventing an argument. "Perhaps that's not the ultimate truth."

How Could Anyone Quibble? It's Such a Silly Word.

Nonetheless, quibbling and belittling rank as the leading evening pastime, after computer and tv time, in many homes around the world. What can you do as Blissologist to minimize, if not entirely eliminate, conflict in your daily life?

☼ _____

☼ _____

Moreover, what is the joyful root of your inner harmony, and how can you nurture this?

☼ _____

Giggling is the shortest distance between two friends. ☺

8

Internal Conversations for Creating Your Joyful Day

Rejoice, Rejoice That We Have Choice

Consciously or unconsciously, we freely choose how we live every potentially ecstatic moment of our astonishing lives, as we continuously respond to the ceaseless opportunities that life affords. ☺

Freedom is the greatest, nearest and dearest joy, especially when we are aware of it. At close introspection, freedom is akin to a glistening, multifaceted gem whose many facets include creational, spiritual, linguistic, cultural, community, familial, mobility, geographical, physical, financial, emotional, social, intellectual, environmental, contemplative, international, ambient, and attitudinal.

How liberating to know that we are completely free, that we do not have to or need to do or be anything, but that we have chosen and continue to choose how we respond to life.

Indeed, we need not be alive at all. Wisely we choose life, and with this choice, we are free to decide precisely how we respond to life's surprises, opportunities, challenges and delights, moment after precious moment. Attentively honoring our inherent freedom is empowering. However, resplendent coauthor, beware: consciously replacing "I have to" and "I need to" with "I'd like to" and "I'd love to" may result in subtle rushes of ecstasy.

It's fun to frequently consider the many benefits of performing mundane tasks throughout the day. For example, why say, "I *have* to go to the bank," when instead we can joyously relay, "I'd *like* to go to the bank," feeling grateful to have money to deposit or withdraw.

Instead of "I need to go to bed now," how about "I'd love to go to sleep now," acknowledging that it's a privilege and a pleasure to go sleep early to feel fresh in the morning.

"I must go because…" (In most cases, *must* we?) It's more gladdening to simply say, "I'd like to complete this conversation now (without an explanation). It's been a pleasure."

Rejoice, Rejoice, We Have *No* Choice!
For What Is the Alternative?

It can be uplifting to acknowledge that we can rejoice when fixing the car, when feeding the children, taking a shower, or tidying the house. We do these things, of course, because there are associated benefits that we sometimes fail to verbally appreciate. Blissologists speak these aloud.

By stating what we appreciate about doing what we do, we claim our freedom and joy. Acknowledging the benefits about each of our activities encourages others to do the same. Consider the following under-appreciated habitual activities and what you appreciate about each.

I need to wash the dishes. ➪ *I'd like to wash the dishes (feeling thankful).*

✿ _____

I have to make dinner. ➪ *I'd love to create a delicious nutritious dinner (feeling inwardly grateful we are blessed with food to eat).*

✿ _____

I have to take a bath. ➪ *I'd relish a bath (glad to be in a place to enjoy one).*

✿ _____

What are three of the most common daily activities that you "must" do? How could you joyfully reframe these? Please state the activity and why you appreciate each.

1. ✿ _____

2. ✿ _____

3. ✿ _____

Freely we choose how much we enjoy each extraordinary ordinary moment of life. Our every activity is precisely as deliciously enjoyable as we decide it to be. ☺

Look to This Day

for it is life
the very life of life
in its brief course
lie all the verities
and realities
of your existence
the bliss of growth
the glory of action
the splendor of beauty
for yesterday is
already a dream
and tomorrow is
only a vision
but today well lived
makes every yesterday
a dream of happiness
and every tomorrow
a vision of hope
look well therefore
to this day
—Anonymous

*May we create news so amazing that it inspires everyone we meet
to live life in such a way as to create their own
awe-inspiring news to share too.* ☺

Questionable Sunrise Questions

Which questions do you ask yourself as you first awaken to the morning? A survey revealed that the following seven questions comprise those most frequently asked upon coming to "consciousness."

- What time is it?
- Is it late?
- What day is it?
- What do I have to do today?
- Why did I go to sleep so late last night?
- Which problems should I try to avoid today?
- What could go wrong today?

These common queries create a silly sense of panic and hurry just as the first beams of naturally happy tender thoughts could be shining into your mind, thereby bringing forth your day in the most glorious way. With awareness, we can wake up joyously each morning. We can wake up consciously and in love with life.

Those who habitually stay awake later than optimum health would suggest can prepare themselves for a dynamic tomorrow by going to sleep before the first yawn. To accomplish this feat, some people initially set an alarm to ring early in the evening to remind them to go to sleep early. By being in bed early, we of course, naturally wake up early with plenty of energy and time without need for an alarm. Besides, waking to alarm is an alarming habit that fills the body with needless fear.

Upon waking, do you give yourself the enjoyment of a few moments delighting in where you are, feeling the comfort of the bed, if you have one, of your loved one, if there is one, and the relaxed pleasure of a few stretches to extend sublime feelings of bedly contentment into the day?

In which delightful ways do you (or could you) particularly enjoy commencing the day?

✿ _____

✿ _____

Conscious Sunrise Questions Let the Sun Shine In

Asking conscious Sunrise Questions awakens wondrous possibilities. These questions are among my morning friends. How would you answer them? Before you do, if you are not already there, feel free to slink back into your bed or a chair, hammock, lawn, yoga mat, beach, cushion or couch to luxuriate for optimal ambience.

What are the blessings of this moment?
☼ _____

What are my ideals, and how can I live them today?
☼ _____

How can I greet this day in a healthy way?
☼ _____

How can I enhance calmness and deepen peace?
☼ _____

What would creativity explore?
☼ _____

What is the focus of my enthusiasm?
☼ _____

What are my highest happiest truths and how can I manifest them today?
☼ _____

What would be the most wonderful experience that could possibly happen today?
☼ _____

How can today be absolutely dreamy, and how can I create this?
☼ _____

What would the Universe like me to do today?
☼ _____

This is the most essential exercise in this book: Borrow from any of the above questions that speak to you and modify them if you like. Create your unique set of Sunrise Questions especially for you to read, consider, and answer upon going to sleep and waking to powerfully invoke a most amazing day every day. After just one morning, you will feel the difference. Guaranteed.
☼ _____

Your Sunrise Questions

When you first awaken, which questions do you most often ask yourself?

☼ _____

☼ _____

☼ _____

☼ _____

What kind of internal ambience of possibilities do these questions create?

☼ _____

☼ _____

☼ _____

☼ _____

Which Sunrise Questions would you ask yourself to consciously inspire a joyous and sacred commencement to your treasured today ahead? Suggestion: keep these at your bedside for a quick peek upon waking.

1. ☼ _____

2. ☼ _____

3. ☼ _____

4. ☼ _____

5. ☼ _____

6. ☼ _____

7. ☼ _____

8. ☼ _____

9. ☼ _____

10. ☼ _____

By asking brilliant questions,
I illuminate myself. ☺

Consciously Creating Your Inner Ambience

We are what we think. With our thoughts we create the world.
—The Dhammapada

How would you describe the personal inner ambiance that you'd most love to create in each of these realms of your sweet life?

Physical
✿ _____
✿ _____

Financial
✿ _____
✿ _____

Emotional
✿ _____
✿ _____

Creative
✿ _____
✿ _____

Relational
✿ _____
✿ _____

Geographical
✿ _____
✿ _____

Spiritual
✿ _____
✿ _____

How can we communicate to encourage the best of
everyone we encounter, including ourselves? ☺

Affirmations for Creating a Most Amazing Day

Affirmations are modern day mantras—positive statements consciously and carefully chosen. Affirmations inspire us to create visions that uplift, beautify, and empower the day ahead. Which affirmations could enhance your life? Which of your highest and wisest truths would you like to manifest today?

✿ _____

✿ _____

✿ _____

When someone asks, "How are you?" which three adjectives would you most love to embody? For example, *"I am strong, brilliant, and beautiful. Thank you for asking. And you?"* Spontaneously answer the question "How are you?" below three times with different sets of exuberant adjectives each time.

I am . . . ✿ _____

I am . . . ✿ _____

I am . . . ✿ _____

The origin of the word "affirm" means *to make firm*, as in affirming your wishes and dreams. Frequently declaring even generic affirmations, such as "Life is wonderful!" and "I love . . . " and "We love . . . " can catalyze what appear to be miracles.

Which affirmations would presently elicit a smile from inside?

✿ _____

✿ _____

✿ _____

If we love life unconditionally,
Life unconditionally loves us back. ☺

Declare Your Day by Giving It Away

Those who say, "Have a nice day," are at a serious risk of having a nice day themselves. Would you prefer a nice day or would you like to live with a tad more *pizzazz?*

An intriguing study shows that neglecting to wish people something uplifting has mixed, and surprisingly, negative results.

In contrast, we can attribute a portion of our unusual amplitude of joy to the wishes that we wholeheartedly convey to whomever we have the good fortune to encounter. Instead of "Have a nice day," how about creating something daringly novel? For example:

- *May your day be blessed by a bouncing herd of wild kangaroos.*
- *Amazing/beautiful/magical/delightful/dreamy day your way.*
- *Supernatural health and strength to you.*
- *May the bliss be with you always.*
- *Much magic ahead.*

What would you like to wish for others that you would love to receive?

☼ _____

☼ _____

☼ _____

☼ _____

☼ _____

☼ _____

☼ _____

☼ _____

☼ _____

Feel free to give these wholeheartedly to yourself, then. . .

Declare the quality of your day by giving it away. ☺

The Spontaneous Glad and Glum List

Understanding the details of what exactly supports our own happiness is a prerequisite for joyous and harmonious communication. To expand into bliss, it's an essential prerequisite to comprehensibly consider how our continuous choices of places, people, activities, lifestyle, food and experiences (and our interpretations of these) affect our lives.

    Without taking into account what you should feel, spontaneously scribble down the names of the people, places, activities, food, and experiences that tend to gladden you on the left, and those that end to render you glum—even if inexplicably—on the right. What are your gut feelings? Stop only when the list is completed. Your answers may be surprising.

Glad List	and	Glum List
✿ _____	✿	_____
✿ _____	✿	_____
✿ _____	✿	_____
✿ _____	✿	_____
✿ _____	✿	_____
✿ _____	✿	_____
✿ _____	✿	_____
✿ _____	✿	_____
✿ _____	✿	_____

On Being an Uplifting Graffiti Artist

In a public restroom, someone drew a large rectangular picture frame where a mirror would normally hang in front of a public restroom sink. Enclosed in the graffiti artist's picture frame, read these words:

Don't Worry, Gorgeous!
You Look Amazing!

9
Empowering Mantras & Energizing Affirmations

Health-Enhancing Communication

What do you think and say (and refrain from thinking and saying) to love yourself enough to ceaselessly create the most stellar health for yourself?

☼ _____

☼ _____

What else do you do (and refrain from doing) to honor and cherish your exquisite existence enough to continuously create optimum health?

☼ _____

☼ _____

Consider a few moments when you felt unusually healthy, strong, and happy. Which factors would you attribute to these moments of heightened well-being?

☼ _____

☼ _____

Approximately how much of your precious time do you enjoy radiant health?

☼ _____%

And Gladness?   And Contentment?   How about Joy?   And what of Bliss?

☼ _____%   ☼ _____%   ☼ _____%   ☼ _____%

What health and happiness-giving habits do you most enjoy? I love feeding birds in my cliff-dwelling bed; wandering barefoot in cushiony woods; singing to and stretching before the rising sun; revering life while being beneath trees; feasting on the energy within the air; swimming in streams, rivers, lakes, and oceans; dancing in dark places with stars, tides, and moon; sharing victuals, vespers, and dreams; giving gifts of words, wild fruits, and love-twinkly gazes; exploring inner worlds; and thanking, forever giving thanks. And you, my friend? What health and happiness-giving habits do you most enjoy?

☼ _____

☼ _____

☼ _____

Universal Affirmations

We *Blissologists* include everybody in our affirmations because your joy is my joy since we are all connected, all hanging out on this tender little planet together. Of course, your well being uplifts my well being as mine does yours. So, it's not only wise, but also efficient, to wish the goodness we wish for ourselves upon everyone else as well.

For example, saying, *"May all beings enjoy harmony, health, and happiness"* is infinitely more potent than merely, *"May I enjoy harmony, health, and happiness."* What would you wish for yourself and everyone else in the following realms?

Universal Livelihood Affirmations

We are discovering our life's highest purpose.
Our work is inspired and inspiring.
We are manifesting our wildest dreams with grace and ease.

✿ _____

✿ _____

✿ _____

Universal Relationship Affirmations

May love flow from my heart to your heart and to all hearts in the universe.
May all beings abide in virtuous, co-creative harmony.
May our relationships grow ever more noble, cheerful, profound and precious each day.

✿ _____

✿ _____

✿ _____

Universal Energy Affirmations

Our bodies are energy temples of supernatural health.
All beings are vibrant conductors of nature's gleeful, vital electrical force.
Limitless and alive, we thrive by freely creating boundless energy.

✡ _____

✡ _____

✡ _____

Universal Prosperity Affirmations

(Did you know that "prosperity" originally meant health?)
We are smile billionaires and living godzillionaires: prosperous, generous and free to be.
We are exquisite embodiments of astounding abundance.
The universe is inherently prosperous, and we are thriving holograms.
Right now, we are easily tapping into the infinite riches abiding within. Prosper forth!

✡ _____

✡ _____

✡ _____

Universal Affirmations for Spiritual Well-Being

Let's activate the miraculous!
May we proceed from the dream outward.
Everything is so divine. Bliss forth with love!

✡ _____

✡ _____

✡ _____

Brimming With Bliss

Imagine yourself as a glass of contentment. If you were such a glass, how full of energy would you assess yourself to be at this given moment?

☼ _____%

Operating from what level of energy is adequate for you? Would 70%, 80%, or 90% suffice? Why or why not?

☼ _____

This is a place for gentle reflection. How would you assess your present level of joy, enthusiasm and contentment in these sunrays of your existence?

Physical well being

☼ _____ %

Emotional well being

☼ _____ %

Spiritual well being

☼ _____ %

Loving life

☼ _____ %

How much am I living by my values?

☼ _____ %

Geographical well being

☼ _____ %

Intellectual well being

☼ _____ %

Creative expression

☼ _____ %

Inner peace and calm

☼ _____ %

How much am I living by my dreams?

☼ _____ %

Which of the above areas are asking for extra love and special attention?

☼ _____

Being genuinely loving, starting with oneself,
is an extraordinary achievement. ☺

Meniscus Meditations

Have you observed that when a glass of water is filled to the brim, a thin layer of water rests above the rim? Scientists call this the meniscus, that bulbous thin layer beyond the rim, the magnetic one hundred and one percent. Anything we do or don't do that replenishes our life force is a *meniscus meditation*.

Like other batteries, the body-spirit requires recharging when low. When feeling depleted, refraining from speaking boosts energy significantly. *Note:* Recharging your body temple battery to full capacity is possibly the most important requisite for sustainable bliss conscious communication, because without glowing health, the quality of communication is often compromised.

How many miscommunications have resulted from verbally exerting oneself when insufficient energy was available? To gather energy, I enjoy luxuriating in delicious spells of quiet solitude, deep celebrated rest, and creative relaxation. Are you a master of relaxation? How do you gather energy to replenish your splendid self? By letting our energy gingerly fill to the brim, drops of energy soon spill over the rim as ready gifts. Since energy is indestructible, immortal, and abundant, omnipresent energy is being continuously replenished.

Mentally, physically and verbally focusing on optimum states of health can magnetize energy and revive our dynamic internal ecosystem, until our body temples are habitually thriving, as these examples demonstrate.

I'm tired. ⇨ *I'm feeling sleepy, so am on the way to enjoy a nap.*

☼ --

I'm sick. ⇨ *I'm cleansing and on the brink of deep recovery.*

☼ --

I'm too exhausted to exercise. ⇨ *I'm about to gently exercise a little to energize my body's battery.*

☼ --

I eat too much junk food. ⇨ *Before eating I ask, "Will this nourish and energize me?"*

An inspired, dream-directed lifestyle, natural nutrition, farm fresh food, fantastic fitness, fabulous friends, creativity and bliss conscious communication result in chronic states of supreme well-being. ☺

The Power of "Wow!"

After asking someone a bliss conscious question, such as *"What's inspiring you these days?"* how can we best demonstrate and exude our enthusiasm for that person? By listening with an attentive gaze followed by an ecstatic "Wow!" Huge is the power of wow.

How can we most succinctly celebrate the mystery and power of the precious people in our presence? How can we powerfully acknowledge those who spontaneously grace our conversations by sharing the depths of their hearts, insights, joy, and discoveries with us?

Are you a *Wowologist*? Interjecting "Wow!" is one of the greatest indicators that we are not only listening, but also listening with our full and loving presence, bursting with enthusiastic support for the speaker's ideas.

Saying "Wow!" is incredibly simple and easy to do. To be a more loving listener, feel free to fill in gaps in the conversation with a power-packed "Wow!" or its relative equivalents such as "Fantastic!" or "Remarkable!" or "Amazing!" or "Bravo!" for more variety and precision.

Which words do you use to exclaim and express "Wow!"?

✿ _____   ✿ _____

I dare you to interject "Wow!" and these other wow-like possibilities much more often in your conversations, even including those conversations that you would prefer to rapidly bring to an end. What happens? What is the power of wow?

✿ _____

✿ _____

✿ _____

"Wow!" means I see you, I hear you, I get you, I grock you.
Thank you, I'm with you.
"Wow!" is the shortest way to say, "I love you!" ☺

Bliss In, Bliss Out (A Meditation Celebration)

"Bliss In, Bliss Out" is a simple, cheer-inducing meditation technique, a boon for literally inspiring groups or your self. While slowly and succulently inspiring and expiring in a gentle soothing rhythm, speak, sing, whisper or think these four simple phrases:

1. "Breathe in" (while breathing in), then "Breathe out" (while breathing out)
2. "Bliss in" (while breathing in), then "Bliss out" (while breathing out)
3. _____ in, _____ out (choose an inspiring word to say, such as *"Love in, Love out"* or *"Hug in, Hug out"* or *"Smile in, Smile Out,"* or whatever inspires you in the moment)
4. Bliss in, Bliss out.

More slowly this time, again:
1. Breathe in, Breathe out
2. Bliss in, Bliss out
3. _____ in, _____ out
4. Bliss in, Bliss out.

Repeat as many times as you like, changing line three to whatever inspires you in the moment such as:

☼ _____ in, _____ out
☼ _____ in, _____ out
☼ _____ in, _____ out
☼ _____ in, _____ out
☼ _____ in, _____ out

How can I be ever more wise, kind, and empowering;
more profound, compassionate and fun;
more helpful to humanity and
to our one shared Earth? ☺

10
Accentuating the Ambience

The Importance of Creating Blissbience

Have you ever moved your couch beside a well-traveled highway so as to better enjoy the thundering, gusty, dusty, aromatic, conversational ambience?
Absurd, is it not? ☺

The environment is generally stronger than we are. For example, if we dwell on a tepid island in the tropics, our wardrobe, diet, lifestyle and outlook will differ remarkably from when we abide amidst high Himalayan peaks in the winter.

Myriad non-human factors impact our conversational ambience such as seasons, climate, sunshine, rain, heat, and cold. Couple these with human-influenced ambience factors such as the furniture, rugs, pillows, windows, views, trees, flowers, gardens, cars, buildings, cultures, languages, laws, education, quiet, clean air, peace, and proximity to nature.

Understanding that our environment is usually stronger than we are, Esteemed Coauthor, isn't it essential that we create and seek out sanctuaries in our immediate vicinities that exude a blissful ambience or *blissbience*?

Where are the pleasantest places to communicate inside your home, and what makes them particularly so?

✿ _____

✿ _____

Are they deliciously cozy, cheery, clean, and tidy? Is the lighting soft and lovely? Do they feature an inspiring painting, an intriguing photograph, an uplifting view or a beautiful, soothing plant, candle or bowl of fruit? Do family and friends naturally gravitate there to casually sink in to the inviting furniture and soak in the exquisite atmosphere, and thusly feel inspired to share awe-inspiring conversations?

✿ _____

✿ _____

Is There a Bliss Conscious Communication Diet?

It can be challenging to thrive conversationally with those under the influence of certain illegal substances. However, the legal poisons that prevail without being comprehensively questioned may be even more insidious due to their widespread prevalence and general acceptance, from pharmaceuticals to pesticides, from junk foods to alcohol to common household toxins. In the long run, these all share common tendencies to dull the mind, dampen enthusiasm, weaken life forec, obscure clarity, and thus, eventually hamper happiness and health, including the health and happiness of our conversations.

   (Un)natural foods beget (un)natural thoughts, and it is thoughts that comprise the roots of Bliss Conscious Communication. Naturally, the more vibrant our foods, the more vibrant are our conversations. Offering unwholesome foods and frequencies to family and friends, including oneself, can derail conversations.

Rather than offering loved ones acceptable toxins such as sugary sweets and caffeinated drinks, what do you like to eat and drink, both alone as well as with family and friends, to inspire the highest qualities in your conversations?
☼ _____ ☼ _____

An ongoing +20-year study at the Happy's retreat, *Heaven On Earth*, observes that a significant rise in Bliss Conscious Communication often results after guests enjoy fresh organic foods and drinks, such as wheat grass juice, wild or garden-picked dark leafy green salads, fresh organic vegetable juices, freshly picked in-season fruits, and glasses of clean spring water since these are *gladness enhancers*. Which foods and drinks tend to add to your energy, clarity, cheeriness and homeostasis the day after you eat them?
☼ _____ ☼ _____
☼ _____ ☼ _____

Before welcoming anything into my mouth, mind or heart,
I ask, "*Will this nourish me?*" ☺

The Jesus Technique

Until relatively recently, nature was the only view available. ☺

Since the majority of humanity dwells in cities, today living near nature is a privilege. In the past, shifting ambiances created while walking, sailing and paddling were the only "movies" our ancestors knew. They created moving movie pictures by moving, as the landscape slowly shifted while each conversationalist experience one lifelong, homemade, ceaseless slow movie of living.

Even today, walking while talking inspires conversations, especially amidst the company of trees. For countless ages, strolling through deserts, along beaches, across meadows, and through mountain ranges has provided *blissbience* for roving conversationalists, friends, teachers, seekers, and sages.

I call cross-country walking while talking *"The Jesus Technique," "The Moses Method,"* or *"The Buddha's Way"* since these and other sages were known to travel great distances while sharing, listening, dialoguing and giving sermons while they walked.

Could your business meetings be more enjoyable in quiet parks along less-traveled nature trails? When on subtropical islands, I have led many staff meetings at beach parks. Office associates tend to show up, participate, and enjoy meetings far more. Establishing outdoor office time at a picnic table is a free perk from your local park that enhances inner peace, connectivity, community, vitality, and joy. Where could you wander nearby your home to inspire ever more *Bliss Conscious Communication?*

✿ _____ ✿ _____

Describe two of the most *amazing places* when you enjoyed two of the most incredible conversations of your life thus far, then please share your observations or hypotheses.

✿ _____

✿ _____

Research biologists say that lead wolves have
the deepest heartbeats and are the most fun.
—Caroline Casey

Celebrating Presence

Let's live as if today is the best day of our lives since today is the only day we truly have. Indeed, the past has left us and the future has not yet arrived. So why long for what has happened or get excited over things that are yet to come? May we squeeze the juicy sweetness out of every succulent moment here and now.

Have you observed how time seems to linger intrinsically in us sometimes, and yet magically appears to disappear when we feel fully alive? Habitually dwelling in "the there and then," (most commonly via defaulting to the Internet, our cell phone, multi media, fretting about the future or pondering the past) rather than living fully in "the here and now" often arises from an unconscious desire to be elsewhere due to restlessness with present circumstances. Meanwhile, life is happening dynamically all around us. Yes, right here, right now, the bliss goes on and on.

The Blissipline of being wholly present entails creating ways to joyously guide past, future, and elsewhere-oriented conversations back to the here and now.

What would you say to encourage time-wandering friends to be fully present with you?

- *How shall we celebrate this great gift, this unique moment in time right now?*
- *How delightful it is being fully alive with you here now.*
- *Listen. Do you hear/smell/taste that? In this unique moment, let's soak it all in.*

✿ _____

✿ _____

To practice shifting the focus to what's here now, how would you gently guide overly future-oriented conversations back to this cherished present moment?

- *Do you think all terrestrial life forms will be transplanted to distant planetoids due to an alien invasion in the year 2345?*
- *What will I be doing in ten years, you ask? What I'd like to know is what will we be doing in 100 years?*

✿ _____

Celebrating Silence

no one spoke
the host, the guest
the white chrysanthemums
—Ryoko

Some sips and tips to savor in the presence of silence:
- *When words end, deep communication begins.*
- *Pausing enhances perception and deepens connection.*
- *Avoid loose speech and those who entertain it.*
- *Character is what you say to yourself when no one else is listening.*
- *Silence is the handiest yet least-employed freedom of speech.*
- *Few people complain that someone is listening too much.*
- *Significant silence begets significant speech.*
- *Which is of greater benefit right now, my words or my silence?*
- *Attentive listening is a bold and beautiful act of love.* ☺

✿ _____
✿ _____

What are your sage observations and feelings about silence?
✿ _____
✿ _____
✿ _____

Better than a thousand useless words,
Is one word that brings peace.
—Buddha, Honorary Blissologist

Conversations are often silent between two wise and loving hearts. ☺

Celebrating Solitude

Sometimes there is nothing so thrilling as the prospect of a date alone with oneself. How un-lonely being alone can be! May you frequently dive into the depths of silence to behold its many-splendored jewels.

as a bee seeks nectar
from all kinds of flowers,
seek teachings everywhere;
like a deer who finds
a quiet place to graze,
embrace seclusion to digest
all you have gathered;
like a being
liberated from limitations,
go wherever you please;
yes, live like a lion,
completely free of all fear.
—Tantra of Z'oquen

Your co-author enjoyed abiding on remote mountaintops for ten years as a forest fire lookout in extreme solitude that I like to call "solitary refinement." The vast solitude was spectacular and surreal. How, when, where, and why do you love to celebrate solitude?

☼ _____
☼ _____

What are a few of solitude's most special gifts for you?

☼ _____
☼ _____

Within the silent grateful mind abides an untold universe
where wondrous discoveries await the open heart. ☺

Enthusiastically Speaking

How would you describe your voice? Is it mellifluous and pleasant to the ear? Is your delivery clear? Do you enunciate and articulate? Is your tone a monotone or do you frequently inflect and vary your pitch and rhythms, thereby creating melodies of enticing speech? Do you speak enthusiastically, emphatically, clearly and sincerely? Is your delivery engaging?

For example, do you *say mornin', Morning, Good MORning, GOOD MORning, good MORNING, or GOOOOOD MOOORNING!?*

✿ _____

How *good* does your morning sound?

✿ _____

When asked, "How are you?" in general, how attentive, clear, sincere, enthusiastic and present is each syllable of your response on a scale of 1 to 10?

✿ _____

✿ _____

✿ _____

Let's experiment with these options, which are best said aloud in the company of friends. Please circle the most enchanting options for you.

Wonderful	What a beautiful day.	It's so good to see you.
WONderful	What a BEAUtiful day.	It's SO good to see you.
WONDERful	WHAT a BEAUtiful DAY.	It's so GOOD to SEE you.
WONDERFUL	WHAT A BEAUTIFUL DAY.	It's SO GOOD to SEE YOU.

Enthusiastic delivery improves posture, deepens breathing, strengthens the heart, and brightens the mind. How do you act differently when you consciously pronounce every syllable enthusiastically?

✿ _____

And how do you feel differently afterward?

✿ _____

11

Wise Words for Sacred Speech

Embracing Your Advisory Committee

Character is formed by the literature one reads and judged
by the company one keeps. —Finis Mitchell

Of 8 billion people, who are your deepest influences and greatest guides today?
✿ _____

Who do you most often emulate and turn to for advice and inspiration?
✿ _____

Why do you esteem them?
✿ _____

What especially qualifies them to be so deeply respected that you heed their wise counsel? ✿ _____

_____

My most important creative, spiritual, philosophical and lifestyle advisors are:

✿ _____ ✿ _____

✿ _____ ✿ _____

My greatest career mentors and inspirational teachers are:

✿ _____ ✿ _____

✿ _____ ✿ _____

My most significant financial and fitness guides include:

✿ _____ ✿ _____

✿ _____ ✿ _____

My most influential leadership, friendship and relationship role models are:

✿ _____ ✿ _____ ✿ _____

Do conversations with the special people named above expand your consciousness and catalyze your growth, joy, kindness, laughter, playfulness, and contentment? Who are a few of your wisest, kindest, most cherished and qualified choices for advisors?

✿ _____ ✿ _____

✿ _____ ✿ _____

Consecrating Conversations

Those who focus on material things, expand into ever more material minds.
Those who speak creatively about divinity, become ever more divine.
See the divine in the material and the material in the divine. ☺

According to your speech, in which direction(s) is your consciousness expanding?

✿ _____

✿ _____

How are you broadening your spectrum of reality these days?

✿ _____

✿ _____

Which inspiring insights are you currently entertaining?

✿ _____

✿ _____

What are two of your most treasured truths?

✿ _____

✿ _____

Assuming that you enjoy discussing inspiring concepts, which intriguing questions could you ask to steer the course of conversation to be most deeply meaningful to you too?

✿ _____

✿ _____

Happiness is a how, not a what;
it is a talent (for being happy), not an object.
—Herman Hesse (and yours truly, Happyo)

Blessology

The art and science of blessing others has been virtually lost in most of the modern world. Consequently, there is sometimes an enormous, unexpressed, sad gap in conversations. This inspires people to go to great lengths to experience its opposite. Some people travel to South America to be blessed by a healer or a healed by a shaman. Others travel to Asia to commune with hermetic monks or to hike high up into the Himalayas with the hopes of receiving a blast of kindness and insight from a benevolent sadhu or guru, while others head to South India for a blessed hug. Countless human beings dream to visit a sacred place such as the Vatican or Mecca or old Jerusalem, all in hopes, consciously or unconsciously, for a blessing, be it from a pope, an imam, a rabbi, or a transformational initiatory experience such as a vision quest or a pilgrimage.

How can we bring blessing each other back into our conversations? Due to the limited, mundane nature of most modern conversations, the vast majority of humanity is starving for spiritual experiences and craving sacred conversational communion. We can save a tremendous amount of needless travel and associated jet fuel, expense, desperate running around, loneliness, despair and disappointment, if only we remember or relearn how to bless each other and ourselves in almost every conversation.

Beloved Blessologist, we can do this! This is possibly our most essential offering. Being a spiritual leader has been taboo for centuries unless you were of a certain gender from a certain lineage. Those days have passed.

I invite you to reactivate your inner goddess, shaman, imam, priestess, wizard, faierie, minister, wise witch, rabbi, angel… or higher self. Blissologists don't bless people by telling people what to do or by sharing a limited interpretation of life. Instead, Blissologists envision the highest, most expanded, outrageous possibilities, then share them; see the greatest good, then spontaneously state it; imagine the most healing balms, then joyfully yet seriously and whole-heartedly offer them up. Every time we say, *"Hi, Beautiful"* or *"Wow!"* or *"Have an amazing day!"* we are blessing people.

How can we deepen and personalize this for every divine expression, for every earth angel, yes, everyone, we meet? As a Blessologist, I hereby give myself permission in every conversation to bless everyone whenever the possibility arises. Do you? ☼____Why or why not? ☼_____How often do I bless or bliss the person I am with? What internal shift is required to exercise your natural talent for being even more of a Blessologist ? May we "Bless Forth with Love" and thereby gently heal our world.

Intriguing Questions for Intimates

Be Ye Joyous Unto Your Beloved. ☺

Is it possible to conversationally approach one's nearest and dearest with perpetual delight, gratitude, sacred play, and wonder? Absolutely! How do you inspire playful yet reverent conversational intimacy in your closest relationships, not only with your Precious Beloved, but also with your family and friends?

☼ _____

Conversations are surprisingly either materially or spiritually oriented. How much of your conversations are creatively or spiritually focused, and why?

☼ _____ %

Marvel-us, awe-inspiring questions are among the most intimate, love-enhancing gifts that beloveds can give to one another. ☺

During the day, do you concoct uplifting, though-provoking, open-ended questions to ask your Beloved? If this is not already your habit, create, then consider asking at least one such brilliant question each day, gradually increasing the number of these questions until they comprise the bulk. Which open-ended, brilliant, uplifting, thought-provoking questions might you gift to your Beloved?

- *How can we deepen sacredness in our communion?*
- *What fosters our moments of most splendid spontaneity?*
- *What can we do to enhance ever-greater conversational intimacy?*
- *How can we invite a new level of incredibly loving, joyfully fun, harmonic living?*
- *Which ambiences, activities, and attitudes most encourage our co-creativity?*

☼ _____
☼ _____

Diplomacy is 90% of a successful marriage.
May you enjoy this book together. ☺

Questions for Creating Community

Not so long ago, tens of thousands of people asked me via an enormous Internet conversation, *"Where do you recommend we go to create community? Where is the most amazing paradise on Earth, and when is the best time to move there?"* They were ready to move and needed an answer from their leader. I realized that for these 35,000 friendly people, as well intentioned as they all are, to plunk down into a paradise would likely change that paradise into something else.

Moreover, we all have different ideas of what constitutes paradise and community. Thus, I suggested, "If you like where you live, stay there. If not, move to where you feel a resonance with the land, the climate, culture, and community. Enhance it, or start your own."

My own words inspired me to immediately start educational, fun, monthly neighborhood evening meetings to create more of a sense of community right under my nose with those living along the nearest streets.

Here are some of the questions that we ask around the circle:

- *What would you like to give to our community and what would like help with?*
- *What can we do to co-create even more peace, harmony, eco-sustainability, mutual abundance, mutual support, sense of community, emergency contingency plans, health, safety, beauty, creativity and happiness in our neighborhood?*
- *How can we encourage and strengthen each other's gifts, dreams & well being?*
- *Does anyone have a need that perhaps one or more of our neighbors could help meet, from changing a light bulb to getting a hair cut to borrowing a garden tool to babysitting to visiting an elder who cannot leave the house? Can anyone offer solutions for this (name the) challenge that many of us are experiencing?*

Rather than ignore them, we can communicate with our neighbors. We can lead courteous conversations with uplifting observations, comments of genuine caring, good news, essential news, innovative solutions, and pleasantries. Not so long ago, when new neighbors moved to the neighborhood, apples were picked and home made apple pies were given to welcome them. Today I gave away our extra tomatoes to our neighbors. Which kinds of questions, comments, actions and conversations create caring communities? What can you do to facilitate this to ignite your neighborhood's community spirit?

✿ _____

12
Priceless Communications

Thing-Free Conversations and Money-Free Talk

If we are prone to unconsciously plunge into the quagmires of materialism, the questions "How much does it cost?" and "How much did you pay for it?" may become perilous conversation-fillers.

Boasting about bargains and inquiring about prices are rarely expansive, though they can be expensive—that is, costly to the quality of our conversations.

If you would like to know the price of something, consider experimenting with the Blissipline of inquiring directly from the merchant, in lieu of derailing precious conversations. May we liberate ourselves from the pandemic of price-fixation.

Complimenting and honoring the human spirit begets considerably more bliss than complimenting human paraphernalia.

For instance, imagine replacing the compliment "That's such a gorgeous dress. Where did you get it?" with simply, "You're so beautiful inside and out."

Consider five common materially focused compliments:

1. ✿ _____
2. ✿ _____
3. ✿ _____
4. ✿ _____
5. ✿ _____

Which related alternative joyous, spirit-expanding compliments do you imagine could shift the focus from admiring each of these things to celebrating beings?

1. ✿ _____
2. ✿ _____
3. ✿ _____
4. ✿ _____
5. ✿ _____

I am an empowering conversational
magnet of the highest inspiration. ☺

Being Priceless

Being price-less is priceless. Can we resist any residual habitual urges to discuss how astoundingly little or how much we paid for our possessions? The modern urban habit of boasting about bargains reduces both our beautiful things and our beautiful selves to pecuniary triviality.

    Refraining from discussing prices and things encourages the opening of a universe of fascinating discussions.

Which topics intrigue, inspire, concern, endear and fascinate you most?

✿ _____

✿ _____

✿ _____

✿ _____

✿ _____

Which queries, insights, attitudes and opening comments could dynamically guide conversations into these directions?

✿ _____

✿ _____

✿ _____

✿ _____

✿ _____

Shower the people you love with love.
Show them the way that you feel.
Things will work out better
If you only will.
—James Taylor

Soulful Compliments

Can we revere the beauty of each soul
harmlessly, humbly and inclusively?
I believe that we can. ☺

Feel free to inspire yourself with the following examples, then create your own soul-filled compliments.

Please experiment by using them generously and frequently for the rest of your loving life.

- *It touches my soul when you share truth from your soul.*
- *What a precious spirit you are.*
- *The resplendence of your being shines through.*
- *How courageous you are. Thank you for beaming.*
- *Your authentic presence is enriching this moment.*

✿ _____

✿ _____

✿ _____

✿ _____

✿ _____

Going within I ask,
"Which portion of my compliments are soulful compliments?"
✿ _____ %

Am I a Human Having or a Human Being?

In the English language it is common, even permissible, to speak about people as if we own them. We often hear people introduce a spouse by saying, "This is my wife." That is considered normal. However, the same person could just as easily have said, "I am her husband," or "We are quite fond of each other," or "Her love is deeply felt," or "This beautiful woman I cherish." Why is it that he does not say these except in very unusual circumstances? ☼ _____

Would you say, "I would like to have a child," or "I would like to be a parent"? By emphasizing *being* rather than *having*, we can, as human *beings*, make our sentences more becoming, less possessive and more intriguingly enticingly.

How would *you* describe two special aspects of your life as having? Rewrite each sentence from a view of enjoying being rather than having, then feel the difference while practicing with friends.

☼ _____

☼ _____

Enjoying Doing

Part of the thrill of being human is our relative mobility compared to trees and shrubs. Doing is *living* life, which can be delightful, so emphasizing *doing* rather than *having* gladdens conversations. Would you say, for example, "I have a guitar," or "I enjoy playing guitar"? Would you say, "I have a garden," or "I love growing a garden"? Though these words appear to differ only slightly, the essence and emotional effects of these approaches differ substantially, especially for your listeners who would be far more inspired learning about your love of living than from hearing a list of your possessions.

How would *you* describe two of your central activities as *having*, then transmute each one into *enjoying doing*? (For example, *I have a pool . . . I enjoy swimming.*)

☼ _____

☼ _____

Cheerfully Letting Go

Today, saying "my house" and "my things" may seem normal since at least half of humanity is now largely submersed in a pandemic of unprecedented materialism.

Nonetheless, and all the more, letting go of claiming ownership enables conversations to take flight into magnificent dialogues of possibilities, philosophies, poetry, humor and music of the spheres.

It's easy to refine conversations and intrigue listeners by simply replacing the word *my* with *the* as seen in the following example.

My giraffe is in my bath. ⇨ *The giraffe is in the bath.*

Please share three common possessive expressions that you sometimes say.

1. ✿ _____
2. ✿ _____
3. ✿ _____

How could you transmute each phrase into something less possessive; thereby, more ecstatically expansive?

1. ✿ _____
2. ✿ _____
3. ✿ _____

Overall, do you own your things
or do your things own you? And why?

✿ _____
✿ _____

I always entertain great hopes.
—Robert Frost

Boasting with Beauty

Self-boasting, as marvelous as it may momentarily feel, sometimes saddens listeners, so cannot be recommended. Those habitually prone to promote themselves can enjoy this antidote: boast about others with equal zeal. One of the most beautiful aspects of loving friendships is witnessing cherished friends compliment each other.

Is the heart of self-promotion competitive or positively unifying or something else? What are the root causes of boasting?

✿ _____

✿ _____

Living dipped in bliss entails a broad perspective of relinquishing winning and losing, since genuine happiness at the expense of another's happiness is unsustainable. We can avoid arousing envy by praising others instead.

May we give credit exuberantly to those who sustain us, possibly including the invisible world, the living earth, and the many earthlings involved. Can we earnestly and habitually seek out the good in everyone and commend all in a sacred, celebratory way even before they may compliment us?

Consider a way in which you are frequently praised. How could you most graciously receive this compliment so that it most gladdens the complimenter?

✿ _____

A pleasant air can be created by replacing what "I'm good at . . ." or "I'm a professional . . ." with "I enjoy . . . ,," then asking what others enjoy to prevent a personal monologue from either party. What, for example, are you talents and strengths?

I enjoy . . . ✿ _____ , _____ and _____.

And you? What do you enjoy?

I'm fond of . . . ✿ _____ and _____. How about you?

What do you love to do?

One of the most beautiful aspects of being in the presence of a happy marriage is witnessing beloveds generously praising each other. Feel free to experiment. ☺

13
Extolling Exceptional People

Most People or Exceptional People?

Most people talk about how *most people* are not living wisely. It's widely known that *most people* spend too much time on the computer, eat too much, exercise too little, work at uninspiring jobs, live by questionable ethics, and often neglect to manifest their loftiest, dreams. So why mention it?

Opportunities are ceaseless for criticizing *most people* who comprise modern humanity at large. However, You With The Blissful Lips Beware: criticism is a form of complaint, so woe be to anyone who entertains such conversations.

Why then is the talk of *most people* so prevalent? Could complaining about *most people* serve as a subtle mans of increasing one's self-image at the expense of society at large? Could *most people* be used as an excuse for one's own mediocre life? Be forewarned: if we speak of or aim for mediocrity, we will reach it, lest we fall short. However, if we aim for the stars, at the very least, we will land in the treetops and enjoy the view.

In lieu of repeating disheartening litanies of how *most people* err, why grumpily complain if we can joyously refrain? Instead, let us focus our verbal offerings on leading the way toward uplifting alternatives and sustainable solutions. What we say about *most people* reveals far more about us than it does about *most people*.

When you talk about most people, would you describe your perceptions as more often critical or complimentary, and why?
✿ --

How much of your conversations are you asking about the person with you?
✿ _____% How much do you spend asking or talking about those who are elsewhere? ✿ _____%   Do you tend to talk more about the ways of most people or exceptional people? Why?
✿ --
✿ --

Most people tend to speak of "most people" whereas
Exceptional people tend to speak of exceptional people. ☺

Exceptional People

To talk of people who live exceptional lives and offer exceptional solutions, one requires associations with primarily exceptional people, if not in person, then in books, videos, or other media. Who are a few exceptional people who inspire you?

✿ _____   ✿ _____

✿ _____   ✿ _____

Would you include yourself in the list? Go on and add yourself. If you struggled to complete the list, consider broadening your social horizons and inspirational perceptions in new, expanded ways. There are about 8 billion human possibilities.

There is a well-known truism that geniuses prefer discussing intriguing ideas; intelligent people discuss events, and mediocre minds most often talk (complain) about people, most people.

According to the above truism, approximately which portion of your conversations do you speak like a genius ✿ _____%, an intelligent human ✿ _____% and a mediocre mind ✿ _____%? (for a total of 100%.)

Dear Co-Authoring Blissologist, let's focus our precious energy on sharing the magnificent discoveries, creations, innovations, contributions, insights, lifestyles, habits and virtues of exceptional people such as your genius self who:
- Are lightning blossoms of optimism, wisdom, and inspiration
- Celebrate everyone's health, happiness, and good fortune
- Enjoy creating ever greater kindness, harmony, and unity between all
- Creatively encourage the realization of everyone's highest dreams
- Enhance relationships by speaking well of others behind their backs
- Thereby contribute to a wonderful world

✿ _____

✿ _____

✿ _____

Perceiving Omnipresent Angels

However we perceive the world, the world usually reciprocates. ☺

For several winters, I dwelt in a jungle monastery in southern Thailand. After the first season of living in the monastery steeped in meditation, prayer, song, scripture and service, I alas stepped out of the monastic hermitage and walked into the marketplace without realizing that something interesting had taken place. To my astonishment, during the course of my stay in the monastery, the ordinary country shopkeepers and taxi drivers seemed to have somehow grown suddenly curiously wise, more magnanimous of spirit and relatively quite enlightened.

Moreover, everyone I encountered was suddenly astoundingly friendly and poignantly generous, as if we had become kindred spirits overnight.

I soon seriously suspected them all to be undercover earth angels thinly disguised in human suits. Many memorable, blissful days passed before I realized what had happened. Perhaps something similar has also happened to you.

Is it possible that by transmuting our own minds, our impressions of those around us may shift, as may their perceptions of us, thus our relations, grounded in an expanded understanding? Under such loving influences, even misguided and professional naysayers may sometimes wake up to their misdeeds, eventually reaching out and ameliorating their perspectives.

In contrast, as our discernment and internal guidance grow, we realize the value of continuing to serve the public in ever wiser ways, meanwhile understanding the essential importance of consciously creating a peace-filled private life with healthy boundaries, choosing to grow intimate familial and professional friendships with very carefully chosen, exceptional people.

What would you especially like to call forth among your closest associates, chosen family and beloved friends? To accomplish this, how could you perceive, then, respectfully address them, thereby calling them into your existence?

✿ _____

✿ _____

14
Can Bliss Exist Beneath Sorrow?

Celebrating Sorrows

During challenging times of crisis, optimistic joy can save lives. Moreover, cheerful encouraging words can surprise our associates into needed elation. How would you tenderly offer uplifting hope, humor, comfort, and joy in these situations? You lost your job? I feel for you. On the other hand, congratulations. Woo-hoo! You're free! May you enjoy every moment. A better job awaits you in PDO, Perfect Divine Timing.

☼ --

Your mother died? Wow. What a huge transition. I feel deeply for you. I'm with you. I love you. Let me know how I can help. She's now on cosmic vacation. How free she must be feeling. Peace and joy be with her. Mystical peace and tender joy to you, too, in every heartfelt moment remaining in your beautiful life. What an incredible and wonderful legacy she left through you!

☼ --

Your car was totaled? And you lived through it! I'm so glad that you are still alive and well. How shall we celebrate our good fortune? What can I do for you?

☼ --

Your former love just moved out? Awww. I love you. I'm with you, you gorgeous amazing extraordinary earth angel and cherished friend! I hope we can enjoy more time together. Could this be an overdue opportunity to discover the exquisite creative and spiritual riches abiding within you that only a little solitude can reveal? What is your new dream?

☼ --

You're sad? Your tears are drops of love, so beautiful . . . you are. May we share a heart to heart hug and conversation? Precious friend, I love and treasure you so very much. You are special to me. You are the best!

☼ --

Sorry Is a Sad Word

Sorry is a sad word. *Sorry* is the adjective of the word *sorrow*. Considering this, the sad, nervous, common, cultural, mindless tradition of saying, "I'm sorry," often brings needless sorrow to countless conversations. In the interest of happiness, let's minimize saying, "I'm sorry," and refrain from doing things that might require it.

"I'm sorry" is considered a necessary polite expression in some circles, especially among many British and New Englanders. Upon approaching someone, well-behaved New Zealand children are often taught to say, "I'm sorry. I hope I'm not bothering you." However, this spreads needless sorrow and botheration.

How can we avoid saying "sorry," thereby giving out sorrow without seeming inconsiderate? For example, how would you approach the following situation sensitively yet joyfully?

Good afternoon. Glad to see you. Is this an agreeable time to speak with you?

✿ _____

Why display pettiness by saying, "I'm sorry," over trifles? If you are three minutes late, for instance, why automatically apologize? Those three minutes may have been passed enjoyably. Most everyone can benefit from the serenity that a few moments of solitude may afford. If we are not habitually late, yet arrive slightly tardy one day, must we call in the national guard of woe and shame? What could we convey instead of greeting our friends with nervous, guilt-ridden sorrow?

"I'm sorry I'm late."   ⇨   *Hooray! Here we are together again. I'm so glad to see you!*

✿ _____

Essential Note on saying "I'm Sorry": *Since hurt can be more rapidly healed by immediately and sincerely saying, "I'm sorry," please say it whenever it can uplift a hurt heart. Life is too short and far too enjoyable to hesitate to love.*

In the wake of any sincere sorrow, may we instantaneously share all the compassion, peace, and gentle kindness we can muster. ☺

Good Grief

Do Blissologists grieve? Absolutely yes, we do - as thoroughly and completely as possible, understanding that only by fully experiencing emotional contrasts such as grief can deep and sustainable happiness be possible. The following quotes are here to ponder for your enjoyment during times of grief.

Are emotions good or bad? Neither. Emotions are designed to chemically reinforce something (it's up to us to find out what that something is in each case) in long-term memory (via pain or pleasure). That's why we have them.
—Dr. Joe Dispenza (and HappyO)

Suffering is not a credential, but an assignment.
Once we learn each lesson, we can move on.
—Carolyn Casey

Suffering can be eliminated.
—Dalai Lama, Honorary Blissologist

The purpose of life is to experience happiness, joy, satisfaction, and peace.
In order to achieve this, much depends on our mental attitude.
—Dalai Lama, Honorary Blissologist

People are often unreasonable, illogical and self-centered. Forgive them anyway.
If you are kind, some may accuse you of selfish, ulterior motives. Be kind anyway.
If you are successful, you will win false friends and true enemies. Succeed anyway.
If you are honest, people may cheat you. Be honest anyway.
What you spend years building, someone could destroy overnight. Build anyway.
If you find serenity and happiness, they may be jealous. Be happy anyway."
—Mother Theresa

When we are aware of it, a strange and marvelous joy abides
beneath the depths of sorrow. ☺

15

The Bliss of Swearing & Embracing Conflict with Playful Glee

The Magic of Swearing

Since words are manifestations of energy, and energy is indestructible, words are indestructible. Where does verbal energy go? It invisibly permeates and re-creates in our environment. Let's now consider the powerful effects of swearing.

In the modern sense of the word, *swearing* is a form of pollution. Akin to dropping litter, somebody will eventually have to pick it up. Imagine picking up the energy of the word *damn*, which means *to curse and condemn to punishment, especially hell*. Swearing is clearly a pernicious pastime that pollutes the very air.

Why then do some people swear prolifically? Those who habitually swear often lack a lexicon sufficient enough to clearly, cogently, and colorfully otherwise express themselves. It is a curious fact that some speakers tend to rarely utter the words *love, beauty, peace,* or *joy*, as if there is a taboo against what is wholesome and kind, though these same speakers may think little of casually cursing. They are likely unaware that *to curse* means *to cast a spell*.

Spelling anything aloud—moreover, writing it out—gives magical power to it. Such was the original enchanting use of spelling that is taught today in schools. The concept of swearing as an obscenity is a relatively recent fad that only proliferated in the 1900s. Even today, twelve of the thirteen definitions of the word reiterate the sacredness of swearing.

Swear

1. To make a solemn declaration or affirmation by some sacred being or object. 2. To bind oneself by oath; to vow. 3. To give evidence or to make a statement on oath. 5. To declare, affirm, etc., by swearing by a deity or a sacred object. 6. To testify or state on oath. 7. To affirm, assert, or say with solemn earnestness. 8. To promise on oath; vow. 9. To take an oath. 10. To bind by an oath. 11. To swear by; a) to name a saved being or object as one's witness or guarantee in swearing; b) to have great confidence in. 12. Swear in, to admit to office or service by administering an oath. 13. Swear off, to promise to give up (something). —*Webster's Unabridged Dictionary*

Which swear word would you like to give up and (when you don't opt for silence) what could you replace it with? ✿ _____

Taking Oaths

An oath is a solemn appeal to the universe or to someone revered in order to strengthen one's determination to keep a promise.

All of us have sworn off of something. What have you sworn off or, better yet, into your existence that has improved the quality of your life? Which are the five most significant oaths, vows or resolutions you have embraced thus far over the course of your life?

1. ✿ _____
2. ✿ _____
3. ✿ _____
4. ✿ _____
5. ✿ _____

How has each of the above decisions enriched your existence?

1. ✿ _____
2. ✿ _____
3. ✿ _____
4. ✿ _____
5. ✿ _____

Which uplifting oaths, empowering promises, or heavenly habits are you welcoming into your high quality lifestyle now? What would you like to adopt into your daily celebration of life?

✿ _____
✿ _____
✿ _____
✿ _____
✿ _____

In full alignment with my healthy, loving habits, my grateful cells
are gleefully dancing and celebrating inside me now. ☺

Inventive Invectives

Swearing is a learned response. Therefore, in homes in which swearing is virtually nonexistent, people are prone to respond silently and proceed quietly, while focusing on solutions, if something perceived as unpleasant occurs. In contrast, in homes in which swearing is considered acceptable, and even encouraged, people often complain loudly about whatsoever they perceive to be negative. Moreover, in homes in which swearing is considered unacceptable, people more often express thanks and enthusiasm for life. Even in challenging circumstances, these folks tend to exclaim humorous, broad-minded, inspiring and insightful perceptions. Such habits evoke courage, delight and harmony.

What are the expressive conversational tendencies regarding swearing in your home?

☼ _____

☼ _____

Since people generally love attention, in homes that swear, where greater attention is given to those who communicate negatively, situations are more often interpreted as negative. The more that complaining is considered acceptable, the greater the likelihood for swearing and destructive drama.

     When we choose to interpret a situation as less-than-excellent, instead of swearing or otherwise complaining, what joyful words can we exclaim? Here are a few inventive invectives for your enjoyment:

- *Good Heavens!*
- *Holy!*
- *Truly!*

- *Preposterous!*
- *Extraordinary!*
- *Ooh la la*

☼ _____ ☼ _____

☼ _____ ☼ _____

Dear Blissologist,
May your every word glow and every syllable shimmer. ☺

How to Help Friends Overcome Moments of Insanity

Shortly after learning of the concept of road rage, a fellow was driving me through L.A. in his BMW convertible with the roof down. It was a perfect sunny day, the breeze was playing in my hair, and I felt content beyond measure as we entered the highway, which was thick with (positively exotic to bucolic me) traffic.

Within two minutes of being in the crawling traffic, my companion slammed his fist down onto the dashboard repeatedly while swearing vigorously for some time. After he alas mellowed to a silent simmer, I asked, "What are you upset about?" to which he said, "I left my sunglasses on the kitchen counter."

Keep in mind that I had very recently returned from many years in Asia where I experienced frequent deaths, injuries, battles, famines, orphanages, and refugee camps. I could not relate to his outburst until it dawned on me that my companion's problem was what I call a "First World Problem." This is a problem of perception more than a dire need.

I thereupon pounded my fist on his dashboard, then started swearing while emphatically waving my fists around and bobbing up and down in the passenger seat, meanwhile creatively shouting out every swear word I could possibly muster. After my enthusiastic tirade, he looked at me and asked, "Why are you so upset?"

I quietly responded, "You left your sunglasses on the kitchen counter."

"That's absurd," he said.

"Exactly," I agreed with a smile.

He laughed heartily. Then we drove in contemplative silence for some time.

He said he's never had road rage again.

How might you apply this playful mirroring approach in situations of your life?

☼ _____

☼ _____

"Communication" returns to its original meaning of "communion"
in each breath of loving awareness and its consequent expression. ☺

16
Ameliorate It!

Euphoric Euphemisms

This is a simple exercise in looking for goodness. How would *you joyously* transmute the words on the left into more lofty and lovable expressions?

cheap   ⇨   *excellent value* or

✿ _____

cold   ⇨   *refreshing, invigorating* or

✿ _____

fat   ⇨   *cuddlesome, chubby* or

✿ _____

old   ⇨   *venerable, experienced* or

✿ _____

lazy   ⇨   *a master of relaxation* or

✿ _____

stupid   ⇨   *somewhat uniformed, a genius in the making* or

✿ _____

I have to pee.   ⇨   *the tinkle fairy calls* or

✿ _____

used   ⇨   *well-loved, pre-loved* or

✿ _____

Which other common words can you creatively convert into something more expansive?

✿ _____ ⇨ _____

✿ _____ ⇨ _____

✿ _____ ⇨ _____

Freedom Is the Greatest Joy.
—Buddha, Honorary Blissologist

Transformational Possibilities

I call upon my inner genius to transcend these beauties into something glorious.

Feeling lousy? ⇨ *I'm feeling a little less than fabulous.*

☼ _____

Our vacation was disastrous. ⇨ *Our time off was surprisingly educational.*

☼ _____

The meeting was a failure. ⇨ *The meeting took some interesting turns.*

☼ _____

You look ill. What's wrong? ⇨ *How are you feeling?*

☼ _____

We disagreed. ⇨ *We are reaching new heights of mutual understanding.*

☼ _____

He's stupid. ⇨ *He's a genius in the making.*

☼ _____

It's freezing outside. ⇨ *Invigorating, isn't it?*

☼ _____

Do can you think of any others that spring to mind?

☼ _____

☼ _____

Funlovingkindness is a most potent change agent. ☺

Freedom Is the Greatest Joy

The very prospect of freedom charms and entices. Most everyone loves feeling free, saying "free," and hearing "free," so feel free to freely add to this free sampling of freedom-enhancing uses of the word *free* to your freedom-expanding vocabulary. Feel free to adopt these, optionally modify them, enhance them, and freely invent your own.

carless   ⇨   *footloose and fancy free* or ✿ _____

childless   ⇨   *child free and easy on the environment* or ✿ _____

deceased   ⇨   *body free* or ✿ _____

divorced   ⇨   *free* or ✿ _____

fruitless   ⇨   *fruit free* or ✿ _____

homeless   ⇨   *home free, mortgage free, maintenance free* or ✿ _____

hopeless   ⇨   *living in the moment, future free* or ✿ _____

hungry   ⇨   *food free* or ✿ _____

irritated   ⇨   *serenity free* or ✿ _____

jobless   ⇨   *free to be* or ✿ _____

penniless   ⇨   *financially free* or ✿ _____

pointless   ⇨   *point free* or ✿ _____

thoughtless ⇨ *intellectually unencumbered* or ✿ _____

How do you love to frolic with freedom? What else makes you feel free?

✿ _____

✿ _____

✿ _____

✿ _____

*Freedom's a flower on Saturday morning
gathering sunshine beside the road.* ☺

Naturally Speaking

Natural metaphors add subtle splendid sparkle to conversations. How would you describe these colorful images with metaphors from nature?

red lips ⇨ raspberry lips or ☼ _____

green eyes ⇨ emerald eyes or ☼ _____

white hair ⇨ cloud-colored hair or ☼ _____

blue skies ⇨ forget-me-not skies or ☼ _____

black fur ⇨ night-colored fur or ☼ _____

orange sunset ⇨ mango sunset or ☼ _____

You smell good. ⇨ You exude the fragrance of jasmine beneath the moon.
☼ _____

You sound nice. ⇨ You sing like a passerine with the beauty of a meadowlark.
☼ _____

I like your voice. ⇨ Your voice is as sweet as a gently giggling mountain stream.
☼ _____

The clearest way into the Universe is through a forest wilderness. ~John Muir

All things share the same breath – beasts, trees, humans. The air shares its spirit with all the life it supports. ~Chief Seattle

Our bodies were made to thrive only in pure air and in the scenes in which pure air is found… One touch of nature makes the whole world kin. ~John Muir

What is your most treasured quote about nature?
☼ _____

Abiding in nature, I thrive with a joyous ease of being. ☺

Moderating the Extremes

Superlatives include *everybody, nobody, always, never, totally, forever, all, none, best, worst, shortest, tallest, biggest,* and *smallest.* Superlatives, unless in jest and play, sometimes detract from a speaker's credibility since superlatives are defined as "extreme and excessive exaggerations."

      Weaving superlatives into one's speech often creates inaccuracies, thereby compromising the truth. For example, if we say, "Everybody always grumbles," does that mean everyone in the universe?

      Emotionally charged speakers may sputter forth superlatives in an attempt to strengthen their arguments. As for me, I would never exaggerate - not in a million years! Giggle hee.

How would you transmute these superlatives into less fanatical, more moderate, therefore accurate, truthful, honest, and inspirational sentences?

You are forever questioning everything. (Twenty-four hours a day?)
I'm feeling like taking a little rest from questions and conversation right now.
The great degree of your curiosity with the world reveals an unusual intelligence.
☼ --

You are always criticizing me. (Always? Even while singing in the shower?)
Sometimes I feel sad after your possibly critical remarks, and I would very much love to share and receive more words of appreciation from you.
Thank you for contributing fresh perspectives, worthy of consideration.
☼ --

You are totally closed-minded. (Without even an open nostril?)
I love that we are both open to learning new points of view.
☼ --

How to soften these superlatives? Please feel free to add your insights here.

always	⇨	*frequently* or ☼ _____
never	⇨	*on rare occasions* or ☼ _____
all	⇨	*oodles of* or ☼ _____

17

Deepening Precious Friendships

Blissfully Listening in the Bath Together

If you have two ears and only one mouth, and I have two ears and only one mouth, could this mean that we are both anatomically created to spend the remaining third of our time blissfully listening in silence together? ☺

May we listen often and audaciously together. In the spirit of adventure, may we make such joyous invitations as: *"Let's listen to life magically stirring around us!"* and *"Let's lounge and listen together."* A wonderful aspect about listening is that we can listen anywhere anytime. We can make listening dates, such as:

"Let's meet in the bath tub at 8 pm to listen and gaze."

Meeting at sunsets, sunrises, or unusual times in unusual places such as rooftops, gardens, trailheads, fountains, cemeteries, or places of natural beauty such as up an easy climbing tree, beneath an ancient one, or on a flat boulder in the midst of a giggling creek can add a glad and romantic charge to our Listening Dates.
        The most profound listening can occur in conversations even when only one of us simply becomes aware that she or he is listening. However, when both people are *consciously listening*, even as each one speaks, something mystical happens—an intimate link of awareness arises and an undercurrent of unspoken joy begins to flow. What are your innovative ideas, inspirations and sage counsel regarding enhancing these aspects of the art of listening?

Places for Listening

✿ _____

Listening Fantasies

✿ _____

Listening Experiences

✿ _____

Listening Insights

✿ _____

Listening Philosophies

✿ _____

Emphatic Listening

Conscious listening dives deep—listening with our hearts and cells, listening with naked toes, listening from great heights, and from the navel of our inner Earth. Listening with quite a lot of quiet, stretches our hearing and listening muscles into subtle realms so that usually imperceptible nuances reveal themselves. With a meditative heart, we can hear far beyond what is considered the normal range of human hearing. Moreover, listening empathetically with full-bodied attention can be a grand adventure into worlds far beyond perceived limitations of individual selves.

Tremendous love, fun-heartedness, presence, curiosity and courage are essential for emphatically empathetic listening as we dance with fearless, open awareness into the perceptions and feelings of others, whatever they may be. Discovering new worlds, we expand our own.

Listening without empathy is not listening, but hearing. If you find yourself saying, "I don't understand her perspective," you have likely heard, though not yet deeply listened with a full heart and an empty mind. Genuine listening evokes consideration, questions, clarification, and deep reflection.

Do you have any delightful prerequisites for deep listening? If so, what are they?
✿ _____

In which situations do you tend to listen with your greatest fullness of being?
✿ _____

In which situations might you choose to sometimes only hear? Why is this?
✿ _____

How can we be, act, or speak so that others will be inspired to gladly listen with the most enthusiastic curiosity?
✿ _____

Active, attentive, empathetic listening is a commonly overlooked,
yet very essential daily practice of Bliss Conscious Communication. ☺

The International Appreciation Game

It is a common and thought-provoking fact that the general populace of poorer countries is usually (unless they are torn by war or cataclysm) remarkably happier than the populace of the wealthiest nations. Why is this? ✿ _____ Here follows a true story that offers additional clues as to possibly why.

Once upon a time, I visited an exceptionally intelligent, though entirely illiterate young indigenous family of nine peasant coffee-bean pickers, two parents and their seven children, who slumbered together on one old, large wooden bed head-to-toe-to-head-to-toe-to-head-to-toe-to-head-to-toe-to-head-to-toe-to-head-to-toe-to-head-to-toe-to-head-to-toe-to-head-to-toe.

These parents invited your coauthor to stay with them in their humble abode (and share their bed head-to-toe) situated amidst a coffee grove that stretched across the slope of a formidable lava-hissing volcano in the hinterlands of Guatemala. Inside their simple hut of wood and brambles, we happily passed evenings playing a simple game while huddled around the fire.

The game begins by gathering two handfuls of red coffee beans from a sack. We then commence taking turns sincerely complimenting other players. With every compliment offered, we give away a corresponding bean. The object of the game is to give away all of your beans.

Although participants may occasionally talk over each other or shout with zest, the game is played with a cooperative rather than competitive air; so relaxation, generosity, and hilarity prevail. Among the smaller children, the game occasionally degrades into choruses of "muchas gracias" (much thanks). The game ends when everyone is laughing and somebody yawns or sings a song.

Interestingly, I've been invited to play variations of the game with various tribal families in several third-world countries. Some people pass feathers, others beads or seeds, but most important of all is the passing of compliments. Try it tonight, if you like, with your family and friends. Feel free to be flamboyant and creative.

What do you observe?

✿ _____

18
Loving Up Our Life Stories

Illuminate Your Life Stories

Personal stories grant us special opportunities to share from our depth of being. Do your personal stories make for precious and uplifting gifts? Our stories unveil our core perceptions. What are the emotional tones of your stories? For the following exercises, please use more paper if you like.

For example, do the stories you most commonly share make you feel (circle as many as you like) grateful, humble, sad, grumpy, glad, bitter, fun, forgiving, amazing, sagacious, or other qualities such as:

✿ _____

✿ _____

What do your stories generally reveal about your friendship with life?

✿ _____

✿ _____

Which stories do you tell that evoke giggle-fond memories or inspiring truths?

✿ _____

✿ _____

What were a few delightful highlights of your childhood that spring to mind?

✿ _____

✿ _____

Which loving gestures of your family or friends have especially inspired you?

✿ _____

✿ _____

What are a few of the deep, difficult wisdom lessons you learned that you cherish sharing out of a caring concern to guide others?

✿ _____

✿ _____

Where was the cradle of your civilization? Which places, people, and experiences influenced your life path and way of being, sparking your unique consciousness?

✿ _____

✿ _____

Your Astonishingly Awe-Inspiring Autobiography

You are a cause for celebration. Your most inspirational, hilarious and wise stories are gifts to be shared. The stories you choose to tell and the way you tell them influences everyone you meet. Feel free to use more paper if you feel inspired to delve more wholly than this slight space permits.

What has been especially delightful, revelatory, and astounding about your chosen life path?

✿ _____

✿ _____

✿ _____

Who have been a few of your most profound influences, and how have they deeply touched and enriched your life?

✿ _____

✿ _____

✿ _____

What gems of wisdom has life taught you thus far? Please share a few central tenets of your sage observations and unique realizations for your upcoming grand life adventure novel.

✿ _____

✿ _____

✿ _____

Would you dare to share a few highlights of your autobiography here? Consider this as the humble commencement of a budding outline for your upcoming autobiographical family heritage keepsake or best-selling inspiration.

✿ _____

✿ _____

✿ _____

If we speak to what is possible
we will inevitably delight and astonish ourselves. ☺

Telling Treasured Tales

Considering the autobiographical stories that you most frequently love to tell, please let one that you particularly enjoy sharing spring to mind. This time, however, as an intriguing exercise in outstanding storytelling, write it from a third-party's perspective, by replacing the word "I" with *she* or *he*, sharing a very brief synopsis of your story here. Feel free to use additional sheets of paper.

✿ _____

_____

_____

_____

_____

_____

_____

_____

_____

_____

Is your treasured tale's new version more, less, or equally as engaging and enticing when told in 3rd person. Why?

✿ _____

✿ _____

What wisdom does this most frequently told treasured tale share, and what is the central ethical, mystical, hopeful, fun or beautiful message that telling this story conveys? Why you tell it? What inspires you from within?

✿ _____

✿ _____

✿ _____

✿ _____

Sharing Original Grins

In wildness lives the preservation of the world.
—Henry Thoreau

Do you freely share wild, fun-loving, and feral truths? For example:

✿ _____

Do you bring up what is unusually, even uncomfortably beautiful? Such as:

✿ _____

Do you mention unmentionable marvels, court cosmic conundrums, and express the ecstatic and sacred, including what may at first seem apparently absurd? For instance:

✿ _____

Beloved Blissologist, do you freely relate unusual, uncanny, hilarious, poetic, solutionary, paradigm-shifting, and/or poignantly preposterous observations? Or would you? A sample, if you please:

✿ _____

We can be magnets of creativity, purveyors of surreal dreams, proponents of tremendous possibilities, lodestars, augurs, visionaries, innovators, think-tanks, catalysts, and even uplifting and treasured troublemakers ☺ who gleefully stir up truths for transformation.

Would you venture to share a few of your most original, marvelous or zany truths, inventions, expressions, theories, hypotheses, solutions, experiences, or perspectives?

✿ _____

✿ _____

✿ _____

✿ _____

✿ _____

19
Creating an Inspiring Future

Future Thoughts

Our dreams and visions are our templates of reality. ☺

What would you love to imagine as three significant features of your future?

1. ✿ _____
2. ✿ _____
3. ✿ _____

How do you enthusiastically envision these manifesting?

1. ✿ _____
2. ✿ _____
3. ✿ _____

About which areas of the future do you speak optimistically?

✿ _____
✿ _____
✿ _____

About which areas of the future do you occasionally speak fearfully?

✿ _____
✿ _____

What and who decides whether you speak ominously or with optimistic confidence?

✿ _____
✿ _____

Accessing the ever-present sage within,
I am free to choose my images of the future and corresponding words wisely now
as I give myself ceaseless gifts of enriching inner dialogue. ☺

Contemplative Commemorations for a Happy New Year

Those who drink at midnight on New Year's Eve are drunk for two years.
Those who celebrate consciously in a sacred way on New Year's Eve are
consciously celebrating and for two years!
– Ajan Po, Abbot, Wat Suon Mokk, Thai Jungle Monastery

How we chose to commence and commemorate both our New Birth Year and New Year's Eve sets the tone for our year ahead. What are some auspicious ways by which you could commemorate these sacred days and nights?

✿ _____

✿ _____

✿ _____

May you give yourself the empowering tradition of writing down the previous year's treasures, lessons and pleasures on your birthdays, anniversaries, and new years as a profoundly rewarding way to deepen your journey, heighten your appreciation, and open up to perceive the bigger picture. Why wait? Would you venture to share a few of this last year's most salient autobiographical peaks, troughs, treasures, and delights?

✿ _____

✿ _____

✿ _____

✿ _____

✿ _____

How would you poetically praise some of the ordinary, yet highly appreciated, blissings (good fortunes) of your daily life?

✿ _____

✿ _____

✿ _____

Transforming our story
we step into our glory. ☺

Happy New You

May you fully honor your spirit for completing another year as you approach your birthday. Here are a few inquiries to consider at any time of year for a Happy New You:

What are a few of your most significant discoveries of this past year?

✿ _____

✿ _____

✿ _____

✿ _____

✿ _____

What have you realized and manifested?

✿ _____

✿ _____

✿ _____

✿ _____

Who have you become? (Which new virtues are you embodying?)

✿ _____

✿ _____

✿ _____

How have your philosophies deepened and perspectives expanded?

✿ _____

✿ _____

How has your relationship with life been enhanced?

✿ _____

✿ _____

If you could, how would you name this past year? This was the year of . . .

✿ _____

How would you name your new year? This is the year of . . .

✿ _____

*I commit to ceaselessly experience the greatest goodness of life
in every possible moment throughout this new year.* ☺

20
Preparing for Your Cosmic Vacation

The Importance of Staying Open with Dife and Leath

A flock of brave souls were having their first lesson in skydiving.
One of the students asked, "What if the parachute doesn't open?"
"That," explained the instructor, "is what's called jumping to a conclusion."

We view death as the opposite of life, as if life is good and death is bad. But death is the opposite of birth, not of life. Life is good and death is equally good.
—Hindu Scriptures

From out of the heart of a dead tree, a sapling shoots up toward the sky. ☺

This intricate relationship between death and birth leads me to wonder, precisely where does life end and death begin? Could life and death together inserparably comprise one cooperative, one organism, one great mysterious dance of birth and death and life and the opposite of life for which we have no word? I call this awareness Dife and Leath.

What are your favorite playful portrayals of the great transition?
- *My grandmother is now on cosmic vacation.*
- *Our illustrious companion was recently liberated from his physicality.*
- *Today she commenced her celestial adventure of ecstatic emancipation.*

✿ _____

How would you most delightfully describe death in your own words?

✿ _____

What would you like to be your departing last words? (And first arriving words)

✿ _____
✿ _____
✿ _____

May our speech gladden and strengthen countless hearts. ☺

Honoring Your Grand Transition

"Making money is easy. It's making a difference that's difficult."
—Tom Brokaw *"And delightful,"* adds Happy.

What would you love to be inscribed as your epitaph, should you choose to have one? It's usually a lot easier to write this now rather than later. ☺

☼ _____

_____

Which songs and dances do you most cherish that would be a perfect farewell to share at your funeral? And, who would you like to lead them on your behalf?

☼ _____

☼ _____

☼ _____

Which poems, prayers and inspirations do you most treasure that would enhance the occasion and deliver your closing message of your luminous life?

☼ _____

☼ _____

☼ _____

What are a couple of the salient features of your obituary? (Please share the essence here to prepare you to expound elsewhere.)

☼ _____

☼ _____

Imagine the most luminous location and delicious details of your funeral. (Feel free to continue writing about these subjects on the blank pages at the back of this book.)

☼ _____

☼ _____

I'm not so concerned whether life exists after death.
More importantly, is there life before death? –Somebody

Fabulous Farewells & Cheery Good-Byes!

What do you say to announce that the moment has now arrived to depart?

☼ _____

Good-bye was originally *God Abide* or "*God be with you.* Today's most common good-bye is "I have to go now. I need to _____. See you later, bye." Sadly, the "good" part of "good bye" is often omitted.

Celebrated Coauthor, how can we generate joy at every parting occasion? Rather than leaving as if each farewell is a small funeral or a pretty escape, how can we part efficiently yet also affectionately and cheerfully?

ABCs to Cheery Good-Byes in 3 Simple Sentences
- Appreciate
- Beam
- Confirm

A) Appreciate attentively.
What a delightful surprise to share a few special moments with you.
I appreciate your enthusiasm. It's been a treat to be in your presence.

☼ _____

B) Beam beautifully.
What a blissing it has been to be in your presence.

☼ _____

C) Confirm dreams prophetically.
It seems your dream of _____ is coming true. I see it happening.
Your future is bright. Awe-inspiring times ahead.

☼ _____

"Conversational Joy" is a muscle of the heart rooted in appreciation. This muscle is best exercised vigorously along with awareness, equanimity, appreciation, honesty and diplomacy. Once we are fit for bliss, life can be, with few exceptions, one long sweet dream. ☺

163

Uplifting After Words

The Blisstionary & Ecstatic Etymology

Dictionaries dance in perpetual transition. Hence, the advent of this Blisstionary, a dictionary of ecstatic etymology and cheery, novel words for blissological posterity mixed with sacred ancient examples to deepen our understanding of the original uplifting meanings of words. Creative new understanding invites a joyous relationship with our mother tongue and, in turn, with our consciousness and each other. Since all sounds are sacred, all languages are rooted in the sacred, when we listen and look care-fully enough.

Addictions—are simply what we talk to people about. Ad = *to* + diction = *speech*; therefore, your addictions are literally what you *speak to* (most often). "What do you speak to?" In other words, addictions are simply the central themes of your conversations. This brings fresh meaning to the word *addiction*, which is decidedly uplifting and worthy of consideration. What are you addictions?

Ah!-inspiring—the possible ancient root of awe-inspiring.

Attention—originated as *attend*, which means to wait and care for. Thus, attention is the state of caring and waiting upon each precious person, opportunity and moment.

Awe-inspiring—inspiring reverence, wonder, amazement and admiration.

Bliss—a subtle state of being in the ecstasy of deep peace, contentment and transcendental joy all at once. *Bliss forth! May the bliss be with you!*

Blissbiance—blissful ambiance. *My aim is to make a blissbiance of heart and mind.*

Blissing—a blissful blessing. *Myriad blissings.*

Blissiplines—the blissful disciplines featured in this book.

Blissology—the study of the Science of Bliss.

Blissology University—the first university dedicated to the study of bliss.

Bliss U—.1) short term for Blissology University or B.U., 2) to bless someone

Blissologist—one who habitually practices the Blissiplines and thereby enjoys consequent moments of bliss.

Blisstubes—blissful Youtubes.

Blisszillionaire—a Blissologist who embodies the Blissiplines; thus, frequently abides in bliss.

Cloud Opera—thunderstorm.

Compassion—literally "with suffering."

Dife—the totality of death and life, existence, and apparent nonexistence.

E-bliss—to eblast something blissful.

Enthusiastic—those who are enthusiastic are literally "in god" because "en" comes from "in" and "thus" comes from "Theos," the Greek god. Whenever possible, it is wise to say "enthusiasm" instead of" passion" since until recently passion had only one meaning—"*suffering*", as in the suffering of Christ or *compassion*, literally *"with suffering."*

Faith is rooted in fate—the goddess Fates.

Forgiving is for giving—forgiving reigns as a supreme expression of generosity.

Funlovingkindness—the greatest change agent.

Gene—the root of these intimately related words: genius, generous, genitals, generate, generosity, genome, gene pool, generator, and genetics.

Gigglebytes—the ecstatic efficiency rating of one's bio-computer. *How many gigglebytes can your system handle? Where are you on your laughometer?*

Glappy—glad and happy.

Godus—god plus goddess = godus, a neutral all-inclusive term for the divine. *Thank godus!*

Godzillionaire—one who is in tune with the godus within, thus lives freely and bliss-consciously. *Certified Blissologists usually enjoy living godzillionaire lifestyles.*

Good—comes from god. *Good god.*

Good-bye—historically, "God be with you" became "God abide" then later became "good bye."

Gorgeous—as beautiful as a gorge.

Grinoobly—grin and ooh; the feeling of a broad smile coming over your face for no reasonable reason, knowing that is going to grow. *She grew grinoobly while sunning and singing at the waterfall amidst wild flowers and butterflies.*

Happy—the adjective that describes the verb *happen*. The root meaning of being *happy* is "*to be one with whatever's happening*".

Heal—to be whole.

Healthy—and holy and wholly also share the same sacred root, thereby uniting what is holy, holistic, and healthy.

Heathen—those who live close to nature, in the heath, a kind of high-latitude shrubbery.

Holy—the origin of wholly and healthy.

Holistic—holy.

Innocence—inner knowing.

Inspire—in spirit.

Intuition—internal teaching.

Invisible—inwardly visible. Interestingly, we say "invisible" not "unvisible" and "inaudible" not "unaudable" because everything is visible and audible when we look and listen within.

Lortunate—lucky and fortunate. *How lortunate to be alive!*

Lovingkindness—kind, conscious, agape love.

Linner—lunch and dinner. *Shall we meet for linner at 3 pm?*

Miracle—a visible wonder or a teller of visible wonders.

Oracle—an audible wonder or a teller of audible wonders.

Pardon— the shortened, modern form of "I beg your pardon," a polite way to ask for someone to please repeat what was said, rather than the rude, "What?"

Passion—suffering. This meaning is surprising. To refrain from bringing on the frequency of suffering to yourself or others, it is wise to use the word *passion* with caution, saying *enthusiasm* instead. Be aware that the root of the popular word *passion* literally means *suffering*, as in the passion (suffering) of Christ or *compassion*, which literally means "*with suffering*".

PDO—Perfect Divine Order. *Everything in PDO.*

PDT—Perfect Divine Timing. *May we meet again in Perfect Divine Timing.*

Prosper—*to make happy and healthy* from the Latin verb *prospere*. The idea of prospering as material riches was introduced in the English language as slang during the industrial revolution.

Psyche—breath. *The psyche of life also blossoms in the psyche of humanity.*

Queer—mysterious, peculiar, odd, strange, wonderful. *How queer the moonlit scene.*

Religion—that to which we give our allegiance again and again, from *re* = again and *ligion* = allegiance. *What is your focus of devotion, your religion of the heart?*

Sacred—*sacrum, sacral,* and *sacrifice* share the same root, inferring that the *sacrum* was originally considered the most *sacred* area of the anatomy.

Sacrifice—to make sacred. As the religions of death overtook the religions of life, the idea of killing as a sacrifice gradually replaced the sacredness of sexual union.

Snug—to cuddle, cozy, snozy, or snuggle up. *Shall we snug up, pup?*

Snuglet—one who snugs up to another snugster. *You beam as the snuglet supreme.*

Snugglology—the science of Snuggling. *Are you a Snugglologist?*

Snugglebuddy—see Snuglet.

(The) Snuggle Puppies— a famous musical act.

Surrender—to literally "give up" (note: it's not *give down*). *Looking up, he surrenders.*

Tour—turn. The root of *tour* is *turn,* thus a tourist is one who turns and then returns home. *We are all tourists on this planet, because the Earth itself is a tourist, ceaselessly touring the solar system that is touring the galaxy that is touring the universe.*

Universe—one word, one verb or one song.

Vitamin G—a nutrient; an essential daily dose of Giggles is medicine for Blissologists. *Have you had a healthy dose of vitamin G yet today?*

Weird—wonderful. If someone calls you weird, perhaps offer this: *Thank you so much for the compliment. You are weird too.* Weird originally meant "wonderful".

Wild—willed. *How is it that wild animals generally have more life force than domesticated? Could this be true because "wild" is the root of "willed"?*

Yesglad—nomad. *Why would you call yourself a nomad when you can be a yesglad?*

We Welcome Your Poetic License

You with the poetic license are hereby cordially invited to contribute to the Blisstionary's Creative Phrases Section. Here is a small eclectic sampling:

• Bliss forth with love!
• Let's activate the miraculous.
• May the bliss be with you.
• Myriad blissings!

An invitation: which of your inventive words and phrases would you love to add to The Blisstionary? Let us know, if you would like your blissful offerings to be featured in the next edition. We would love to expand this fun, wee compendium of uplifting phraseology as a group project with co-authoring Blissologists. Feel free to bliss forth your delightful definitions and ecstatic examples via emailing happy@happyoasis.com to be featured in the next edition. www.HappyOasis.com
☼_____ ☼_____

Poetic Activists

Bliss Conscious Communication is not limited to verbal conversations. As the coauthor of our book, I hereby invite you to join the plethora of Blissologists who are creating a more fun, loving, and beauty-full planetary ambiance by spontaneously and respectfully broadcasting uplifting parables, endearing quotations, sweet jokes, love notes, empowering paintings, lyrics, sonnets, songs, beatific multi-dimensional creations and poetic inspirations on public notice boards, refrigerators, mirrors, doors, walls, windows, sidewalks, dashboards, clothes, websites, telephone posts, trees, text messages, videos, backs of street signs, fountains, fences, shrubbery, shoes, rocks, noses, hats, cardboard boxes, tv and radio shows, and other prominent and poetic places with pens, crayons, pencils, paint, computer graphics, natural objects, even recyclables, exploring an infinite array of creative multi media possibilities.

169

The Story of Happy's Name

Out of curiosity people often ask about my name. Many assume that my parents were hippies. Others imagine that my parents were simply o so happy about my birth because I must have I slid easily out of the womb while smiling, singing and dancing. Not true. It was an unusually difficult birth, and the real story that birthed Happy Oasis is far more intriguing.

As a child, I was fascinated by the free spirits of remote tribal peoples who were featured in *National Geographic* magazines, people whose stories inspired me to seek out the few remaining tribes who were still living natural ways in order to glean their wisdom, feel their kinship with the earth, and learn their ancient ways.

At sixteen, I received a scholarship to study Intercultural Studies at Hobart Matriculation College for a year in Tasmania. That year was a culturally eye-opener. At eighteen, after another year of university back in the USA, I set again off for what would begin a lifelong journey as the world's first self-proclaimed "Adventure Anthropologist."

By the time I was nineteen, I had backpacked and worked my way through the backwaters, jungles, and high mountains of several Asian countries, to arrive at midnight in Dhakka, the capital of Bangladesh, in the midst of what I discovered to be a seriously-torrential, month-long monsoon rainstorm.

Several people seemed to be sleeping in the dark beneath soggy thin blankets in the pouring rain on the sidewalk in front of my dilapidated hotel. However, the next morning, watching the many skinny, bare-footed businessmen scurry around and hop over them, I realized that those still-sleeping people covered by sheets were, in actuality, dead. (Yes, they were liberated and on cosmic vacation.)

I decided to cash some travelers' checks and board the first bus out of there to head in the direction of the Khasi hill tribe with whom I wished to live and learn. These Khasis were living in the then remote Chittagong Hills in what was then a deep forest at the edge of what was then a large and lovely lake by name of Sylet.

The rain kept pouring, furiously so. A while after our departure, the bus came to a sudden halt in the raised highway just after I heard what sounded like two thunderous trains, one running in front and the behind our bus. This is when a rushing torrent of water spilled over the rice paddy, hitting the banked side of our raised road, thereby creating a whirling pool, which welled up and streamed over some of the road.

This spontaneous sudden stream, which had appeared from out of nowhere, then started gnawing into the dirt that was supporting the sides of the road. It soon grew into a wild, churning river where moments before there had been only flooded rice paddies. Apparently, a dam had burst further inland.

All the men stepped out of the bus and started talking rapidly in animated Bengali among themselves. I was the only woman remaining on the bus. As a woman in a Muslim country, I sat at the far back row of the bus with a burkah draped over my head.

Through the window beneath the steadily pouring rain, I saw many people standing and walking around the bus outside, several of them carrying sick, sleeping, dying, or dead children in their arms.

Everyone was skinny and seemed to be starving. I wondered how to help. I first thought to exchange all of my travelers' checks. However, out here in the countryside, there were no banks. I then thought to buy everyone a meal, to stave off the hunger, with all the Bengali money that I had, but then realized that there was no food available to buy. I was feeling useless to a point of frustration when a man walked up to me through the rain beaming a big grin on his thin face.

"How can you smile in a circumstance like this?" I asked upset, forgetting that in Bangladesh English is a second language.

"Madam," he answered in perfect English with a Bengali accent, grinning even more. "Smiling is all I have to give. Come, Come with me," he suggested in an inviting yet authoritarian voice.

I realized that this smiling man was a highly educated community leader, some kind of professional and an elder at the young age of approximately thirty-three.

The smiling man stomped his foot into a puddle, clapped his hands, and commanded me to sing a song. "But I don't sing," I protested, at first.

In such circumstances, he could not hear "no."

For the next several hours in the pouring rain, we sang drenched above the mud to one starving child after another, the smiling man on one side and me on the other. I sang Christian summer camp songs; the smiling man sang hauntingly beautiful songs to Allah. We would sing until each dying child's desperate frown would seem to change ever so slightly toward a crying glance, even a slight smile, then we'd sing a little longer or move on.

As dusk approached, it dawned on me that I hadn't eaten all day. I felt a gnawing hunger grow as I started to realize that I would likely not get out alive. I was a member of Amnesty International. Amnesty was of no avail. I considered the Red Cross. No helicopter could find us in this relentlessly pouring rain. Nobody would be coming to save us. It dawned on me that this situation could be widespread across the entire country and possibly beyond. I felt hopeless.

As the water continued to rise, I saw my short 19-year life flash before me—hundreds of random poignant images—then understood it to mean that I was about to die. Meanwhile, the churning rivers were still cutting into the side of the road both in front of our bus and behind it, encroaching ever closer until at some point, the entire section of the road we were on would be consumed by the rising waters.

For a strangely peaceful moment, I accepted that death was inevitable. Then I snapped out of this acceptance of death, noticing that I was the only foreigner, that I had just stepped (bussed) into this scene, that it was not necessarily my fate to die in a flood in Bangladesh, and that, therefore, maybe I could step out of it.

Instead of praying to any intermediaries including Jesus, I tried a more direct approach to cut a deal directly with God, Godus, Allah, Shiva, the Big It, or whatever else different cultures call the Universal Energy Field.

I solemnly pleaded to the Universe, "I will stop complaining if I can live!". I vowed in whining, tearful tone imbued with desperation and a masked complaint. The rain responded by pouring harder. I gathered myself and tried again, determined to inspire some kind of miracle.

"If my life is somehow saved, I vow that for the rest of my life, whenever I am in a circumstance that is any less dire and difficult than this, I will be like this smiling man. For the rest of my life, I vow to be a Happy Oasis unto the world."

Thanks Be to You

Thanks Be to the Spirit of The Universe for the Ceaseless Surprises, Wondrous Gifts, and Delicious Magic Inherent In Each Moment; For Sacred Silence, Earthlings, Ancients, Understanding, Moonbeams, Energies Within Ethers, Compassion, Thanks For Writing This! Kudos To You Vortexing Vibrations, Ecstatic Heart Twirls, Luminosity, Children, Elders, Ancestors, including Chlorophyll, In(wardly) Visible Universes, In(wardly) Audible Worlds, The Eternally Dancing Light Show of Subatomic Particles, Our Cryptic Beatific Origins, Marvelous Mother, Delightful Dad, Brothers, Sisters, Mystic Whispers, Limitless Possibilities, Tall Trees, Truth, Gumption, Prayer, Cotyledons, Chloroplasts, Sunshine, Health, The Invention of the Spoon, Simplicity, Swimming, Fresh Yet Ancient Wind, Dife & Leath, Smiling, Grinning, Nectarian Words & Worlds, Hugs, Mist, Kindness, Tenderness, Tears, Inspiration and Other Gifts of Being; Oneness, Godus, Mountains, Shiva, Genius, Brooklets, Wildness, Mildness, Meadows, Mosquito Gurus, Deep Peace, Humming, Fauna Families, Singing Passerines, Siblings Submarine, Rainbows, Tingling in Perpetual Awe, Attention Crystalline, The Capacity To Wonder, Thriving, Inspired Creativity, Devotion, Innovation, Bhajans, Blossoming, Bodhisattvas, Twilight, The Untamable, Transmutation, Feral Arugula, Satsang, Skipping, Singing, Courage, Weirdness, Prasad, Equinimity, Internal Paradises, Havens of Well-Being, Revelations, Illumination, Emerald & Saffire Seas, Idiosyncrasies, Sacred Forests, Now Sweet Now, Sweet IS, The Living Loving Universe, The Humble Miracle Called Soil, Sangha, Mangoes, Compost For The Soul.

Thanks Be to every Treasured Human Sister and Brother with Extra Special Thanks To Aeoliah, Aeon, Alaya, Aletha, Alexa, Ananda, Angel, Ani, Allowah, Anahata, Asha, Aya, Barbie, Beloved, Bobby, Cat, C.C., Cici, Coco, Daniel, Danette, Dane, David, Dennis, Ed, Elizabeth, Ember, Eric, Fantuzzi, Foster, Gabriel, Gary, Heidi, Human, Jack, Jean, Joel, John, Jonathan, Judy, Kat, Katrina, Katharine, Kevin, Kimberly, Kit, Linda, Lisa, Liz, Lyn, Larisa, Laura, Manis, Markus, Marti, Martin, Mia, Micah, Michael, Miguel, Oman, Oprah, Osha, Peter, Porangui, Precious, Ram, Rangita, Rose, Rysheak, Sara, Saratone, Sequoia, Shambala, Shareen, Sharon, Sharyn, Shawn, Sher Shah, Sky, Stephanie, Swami, Tina, Tony, Uqualla, Vivek, William & supreme Gladitude with Big Love for my best friend, beloved & co-adventurer, John Light. Infinite appreciation to Sages, Sadhus, Wise & Loving Aspirants, Mystics, Musicians, Ascetics, Truth Gurus, Beloveds, Hermits, Fairies, Elements, Wave-Particles, Space, People of Peace, Beings & Nonbeings, Past-Present-Future Precious Mysteries Including You, Rainbows Alive In Drops of Dew, and First and Most and Last of All, Life, Galaxies of Gratitude to the Cosmic Conscious, Blissful, Giggling, Fun, Loving, Kind Communion Which Sustains Us. I Love You All.

Thanks Be to You
(Your Acknowledgments)

☼ _____

_____

_____

_____

_____

_____

_____

_____

_____

_____

_____

_____

_____

_____

_____

_____

_____

_____

_____

_____

_____

_____

_____

Life isn't about finding yourself. Life is about creating yourself.
—George Bernard Shaw

Blissology University & The Bliss U News

At Bliss U, we believe that everyone deserves a degree of Bliss. - ☺

Blissology University is affectionately called Bliss U (as in *Bliss You!*) and B.U. (as in *Be You!*). Bliss U is world's first university solely dedicated to researching the causes of bliss, introduce the Blissiplines, and certify Blissologists with Degrees of Bliss. www.BlissologyUniversity.com

      Founded in 2013 by Happyo, Blissology University has graduated thousands of students who are certified as Budding, Blossoming, or Blooming Blissologists. B.U. also offers corresponding certificate classes in topics such as Certified Pragmatic Ecstatic, Certified Succulent Strategist for Supernal Health, and Certified Lifestyle Godzillionaire. Students may earn degrees and receive Student IDs from Blissology University while enjoying courses and seminars in person and online.

Graduate Blissologists are now being invited to become the world's first certified:
- Bliss Conscious Communication Consultants
- Health & Happiness Consultants
- Blissful Life Consultants
- Certified Teachers in Bliss Conscious Communication

Bliss U invites you to an ecstatic array of additional Blissology classes such as:
- Living Your Godzillionaire Lifestyle
- Living Free in an Unfree World
- Ecstatic Etymology
- Fundamentals of Funology
- Succulent Strategies to Supernatural Health
- The Ecstasy of Ethics

Please email us your treasured tales and testimonials!
Nothing expands our possibilities so much as limit-free thinking. ☺

Many of these Inspiring Friends are Guest Professors at Blissology University, or B.U.

It's an honor to be blessed with so many magnificent friends, exemplars who are creating a more wonderful world. With deep gratitude and enthusiastic praise I present to you a few:

Aeoliah www.MusicforHealthyLiving.com Aeoliah's exquisite angelic art, books and innovative music of the celestial spheres have endeared millions of fans.

Alexa Sunshine Rose www.AlexaSunshineRose.com Her soulful, heart-awakening, beauty-full folk music evokes blissful delight.

Anahata www.ShamangelicHealing.com Anahata's unique, spontaneous, expansively-poetic, personalized insights and shamangelic healings also integrate soothing massage.

Asha Deliverance www.PacificDomes.com Inspired by her mentor, Buckminster Fuller, Asha incorporates principles of Blissology, sacred geometry, and alternative science into to her *Pacific Domes*, the world's leading portable, state-of-the-art domes.

Aya www.Starwheels.com This French diplomat turned yogi, artist and gardener, has created giant celestial mandalas based on sacred geometry as well as brilliant books of playful poetic inspirations.

Bethy Love Light www.BethyLoveLight.com This free spirit Bethy masterfully weaves celebration into our lives via Muzoetry, her first world music cd with blithe lyrics and soulful melodies.

Brigitte Mars www.BrigitteMars.com Brigitte is renowned as Boulder, Colorado's most celebrated health researcher, prolific author, uplifting Naropa Institute professor, and fresh vibrant vegan chef.

Chris Spheeris www.ChrisSpheeris.com Grins grow upon delving into his mind-expanding films, provocative poetry, beatific, photography, film, art and spicy, humorous, love-filled music.

Dennis Kucinich Congressman Kucinich was the main champion of the Bill to create a U.S. Department of Peace. He courageously continues to be a compassionate force for social justice, health justice, world peace and sane environmental policies alongside his equally-inspiring wife, Elizabeth Kucinich.

Devaa Haley www.Devaa.com Devaa's philosophy of kindness and healing presence are a boon to *The Shift Network* that creates frequent on-line conferences featuring renowned luminaries.

Don Miguel Ruiz Jr. www.donMiguelRuizJr.com Carrying on the ancient Toltec lineage from his father, don Miguel Ruiz Jr (author of *The Five Levels of Attachment* and *Living A Life Of Awareness*) is a fun loving and dynamic performer who lights up the room wherever he speaks.

Don Miguel Ruiz Sr. www.donMiguelRuiz.com This kind hearted, strikingly friendly Toltec wisdom keeper has inspired millions through his books *The Four Agreements*, *The Way Of Love* and now through passing his lineage to his sons.

Dr. Brian Clement & Dr. Annamaria Clement www.HippocratesInst.org Co-directors of the USA's most comprehensive, cutting-edge, medical healing facility and health resort in West Palm Beach, FL, these brilliant authors are ebullient, engaging, mind-expanding, health-science presenters.

Dr. Elizabeth www.DrElizabeth.com Author of *Skinnydipping in the Fountain of Youth*, Dr. E is a fitness inspiration, Blissologist & Youthologist.

Dr. Jacob Liberman www.JacobLiberman.org Dr. Liberman. This conscious optometrist, expansive meditator and phenomenal presenter is the eye-opening author of *Light: Medicine of the Future, Take Off Your Glasses and See* as well as *Wisdom From an Empty Mind*.

Dr. Richard Anderson www.AriseAndShine.com Renowned as a medical researcher, nutritionist, iridologist, professor, herbalist and author of *Cleanse & Purify Thyself,* Dr. Anderson also created *Arise and Shine* herbal cleanse products, accredited for having sparked the internal cleansing movement into it's present trend.

Dr. Gabriel Cousens www.DrCousens.com and www.TreeOfLife.nu Author of numerous breakthrough books about live vegan foods, overcoming diabetes, and spirituality, Dr. Gabriel Cousens founded *The Tree of Life* in Patagonia, Arizona. He also leads international humanitarian projects and retreats around the world.

Dr. Jameth Sheridan www.HealthForce.com This cutting-edge naturopath, health researcher and author continues to create numerous nutritionally dense, organic, herbal, superfood formulae for America's health conscious populace.

Elizabeth Kucinich Executive Producer of the award-winning film, OMG GMO, and wife of Congressional Representative Dennis Kucinich, Elizabeth is rising as one of the most endearing, brilliant and powerful environmental and social justice activists in the USA.

Fantuzzi www.FantuzziMusic.com One of this planet's most fun loving, vibrant, and wise bards, this inter-culturally rich and joyful troubadour of sacred music and celebration, was inspired to create his hit song and cd *Ease & Grace* from a poem by Happyo.

Gangaji www.Gangaji.com An insightful spiritual sage, Gangaji is a loving author and empowering teacher who inspires a deep presence that often leads to bliss.

Gary Zukav & Linda Francis www.SeatOfTheSoul.com Meet two of the world's best selling spiritual authors who most recently co-authored *Spiritual Partnership* as well as the 25th anniversary edition of *Seat of The Soul* featuring forwards by Oprah and Maya Angelou. With a long and illustrious career as both a presenter and an author, Gary Zukav is also a frequent guest on Oprah.

Gypsy Soul www.GypsySoul.com This dynamic, soulful musical duet's deeply-moving music tantalizes the heart and inspires us into ever more loving action.

Jean Houston www.JeanHouston.org Powered by gumption, caring, curiosity and transformational fun, this worldly, outspoken leader and eminent author known as Jean Houston has guided countless searching souls to fulfill their greatest potential.

John Light www.GlobalSourceCenter.com This renaissance man is a brilliant researcher, explorer, builder, singer songwriter, performer, true friend, treasured co-adventurer and my beautiful, heartful, precious beloved. John is the founder of the Global Source Centers, local online communities that connect conscious evolutionaries. He produced numerous beauty-full cds and is the educator who wrote many tomes including the *Global Sovereign's Handbook*, a perennial classic.

Kimberly Carter-Gamble & Foster Gamble www.ThriveMovement.com This exceptionally compassionate, kind and generous couple are inspiring people from around the world to work wisely together and act vigorously on peacefully and creatively solving today's challenges. They co-produced the movie Thrive that has gone viral among tens of millions of viewers thus far.

Katrina Blair www.TurtleLakeRefuge.org Durango, Colorado's renowned environmental solutions leader, Katrina, the founder of *Turtle Lake Refuge*, is also a natural Blissologist, researcher, organic farmer, singer, songwriter, fun-loving ecological teacher and author of her newest, *The Wild Wisdom of Weeds*.

Kedar St. John www.TempleofPeace.com Kedar is the cheer-inducing, happy reverend who with his wife Shelley, co-created the *Temple of Peace* where they lead playful and profound interactive Sunday Heartsong Services as well as classes and workshops for the Maui community.

Larisa Stow www.LarisaStow.com An embodiment of bliss, Larisa is a sought out singer-songwriter who weds classic rock with spirituality, and weaves philanthropy with fun. Her music evokes reverence and wonder while inspiring audiences to dance, pray, and sing along.

Marci Shimoff www.HappyForNoReason.com This celebrated transformational leader authored the #1 *New York Times* bestselling book *Happy for No Reason*, which features the inspiring story of Happy's name called "The Smiling Man" on pp. 266 – 268. Marci coauthored six of the top-selling titles in the *Chicken Soup for the Soul* series and was a featured teacher in the international movie and book sensation *The Secret*. *Love For No Reason* is her most recent bestseller.

Meenaskshi Angel Honig www.AngelYoga.com A former personal secretary to Swami Satchitananda, Angel is Maui's inspirational yogini, classic yoga teacher, vegan, effervescent author and Blissoligist.

Mia Margaret Angelica www.SedonaSourceCenter.com/profile/miamargaret Angelic harpist and uplifting author, Mia may be the most conversationally-gifted, joy-generating Blissologist we know.

Michael Beckwith www.AgapeLive.com/michaelbeckwith Founder and reverend of southern California's vibrant congregation, Agape International, Michael authored numerous empowering books. Reverend Michael Beckwith is one of the USA's most dazzling orators and celebrated Blissologists who was featured in *The Secret* and on *Oprah*.

Michael Modzelweski www.MichaelModzelewski.com Ardent Blissologist, Discovery Channel host, author, celebrity, frequent Oprah guest, and international extreme Adventurer, Michael is the Show Naturalist on Princess Cruises Alaska and Africa.

Mirabai Devi www.MirabaiDevi.org This elegant and kind-hearted South African spiritual teacher, mystical author and presence, now teaches and resides on the island of Kauai.

Murray Kyle www.MurrayKyle.com Murray is a joyous, earth-loving Australian singer and enchanting songwriter whose sagacious, haunting lyrics beckon ancient wisdom for today.

Oprah Winfrey Need I say more? www.Oprah.com

Ram Dass www.RamDass.org One of the most intelligent, loved, and fun-spirited spiritual teachers of our times, Ram Dass traveled to India in the 1960s, then authored the classics *Be Here Now* and *Be Love Now*. A venerated elder, today Ram Dass continues to teach and celebrate life on Maui.

Ricki Byars Beckwith www.RickieByarsBeckwith.com A Revered singer-songwriter whose transcenedent music opens the heart, touches the soul, and uplifts the spirit.

Sarah McLean www.SedonaMeditation.com This adventurous international traveler authored *Soul-Centered: Transform Your Life in 8 Weeks with Meditation*. Sarah is an inspiring, contemporary meditation teacher who makes meditation accessible to everyone. The founding program director of The Chopra Center for Wellbeing, Sarah now directs the McLean Meditation Institute for transformative meditation training in Sedona, Arizona and beyond.

Stephanie Sutton-Flanagan www.PhiSciences.com Generous, creative and compassionate, this researcher and psychotherapist founded Planet HeartWorks, a think-tank for fostering global interactive connectivity. Member of the West Wolf Medicine Society, the Cherokee nation of Indians and Chair of Flantech Asia-Pacific, Stephanie also helps steer the work of her husband, Dr. Patrick Flanagan.

Steve Bhaerman (Swami Beyondananda) www.WakeUpLaughing.com
The USA's most beloved cosmic comedian, Steve has one of the most brilliant, witty minds of these times. Mariannie Williamson called him "The Mark Twain of our generation." Swami's comedy has been described both as "comedy disguised as wisdom" and "wisdom disguised as comedy." With coauthor Bruce Lipton, *Spontaneous Evolution* is his most recent book.

Viktoras Kulvinskas www.Viktoras.com An adept Blissologist, Viktoras is the innovative scientific health researcher who was a catalyst for the sprouting evolution of the 1970s and a cofounder of Hippocrates Health Institute. Author of the worldwide bestseller *Survival Into the 21st Century* as well as several other books, Viktoras still travels extensively to teach arcane treasures of health.

Certificate of Bliss

Blissology University

Hereby Celebrates _____
As A Certified Budding Blissologist, CBB

Whereupon it is agreed that This Certificate Course is only entirely achieved when the Certified Budding Blissologist _____
joyfully and completely co-authors every page of _____'s
unique version of the requisite course book,
"Bliss Conscious Communication" and practices the Blissiplines within.

We believe that everyone deserves a Degree of Bliss
Congratulations. We Celebrate You.
May The Bliss Be With You As You Activate The Miraculous.

Bliss Forth With Love,

Happy Oasis _____
Dated _____

Bliss U   www.BlissologyUniversity.com

About the Author

Affectionately called "Happyo", Happy Heavenly Oasis is a lifelong Yesglad. [She asks, "Why be a nomad when you can be a yesglad?"]

Adventure Anthropologist and Blissologist, Happyo, has been slowly and succulently exploring the planet for decades, mostly out of a backpack, seeking wise, kind people of the earth. In the course of her anthropological adventures, Happy was adopted by several sage and loving tribal families in numerous remote, now-historic paradises in many nations during her decades abroad. Most of these tribal families were killed in battles, genocide attempts by governments to obtain their land, so Happy served in refugee camps and orphanages with those who remained alive.

Wisdom-seeking Happyo gleaned these indigenous peoples' blissful ways of communicating even during great challenges. Their courageous and magnanimous cheer inspired both this book and her JOB (Joy of Being) as the *Visionary Blissologist* of Bliss U (Blissology University), with a mission to inspire ever more empathy, lovingkindness, harmony, peace, bliss, creativity, health and happiness on our precious planet that we all share and steward.

A self-trained international environmental advocate, Happy has won seven major eco-cases in court thus far. Deemed a pragmatic ecstatic, comprehensivist philosopher, ethical advisor, human rights advocate and community leader, Happyo is also a poet, eco-entrepreneur, innovator, athlete, artist, gardener, songwriter, circle singer, linguist and wilderness guide. At 16, Happyo received a scholarship to study at Hobart Matriculation College in Tasmania for an eye-opening year of intercultural, philosophical, political and environmental studies.

After thriving as a self-funded teenage eco-entrepreneur and English teacher, exploring Asia's hinterlands and volunteering with tribes for several years, betwixt trekking seasonally through Nepal and India's Himalayas, Happyo returned alas to the USA years later to be certified by NOLS (National Outdoor Leadership School) as a mountaineering guide via University of Utah.

While serving as a forest fire lookout for the Forest Service (USDA), she would return from six-month winters abroad back to the USA each spring to live alone for ten six-month summers in a series of very remote forest fire lookout towers accessed by long hiking trails leading to the tops of mountaintop homes amidst the hidden, little known, verdant, cool, seasonal alpine monsoon rainforests of north central Arizona. From these fire lookout towers Happy graduated with honors from NAU with a full scholarship and personalized instruction in Biology, Religious Studies and Cultural Anthropology. Some of the bravest professors agreed to hike up to her mountaintop, one by one, amidst mountain lions and bears, to teach her.

Happy worked as a director and meditation teacher at Thailand's largest tropical jungle monastery, and later as the show time photographer-naturalist-choreographer-anthropologist-performer (the ship's main act) on a Princess Cruises ship throughout Alaska's Inside Passage.

She has been a performance poet in New Zealand, a trekking guide in the Himalayas, an elephant guide in Thailand, an English teacher for heads of Asian governments, and the visionary founder of Raw Spirit, the world's preeminent vibrant (raw) vegan, health, music, eco, peace, compassion, joy and lovingkindness festival.

This peripatetic poet also authored the national #1 best-selling poetry book in New Zealand - *uncivilized ecstasies*, a passport-sized book of nomadic, ecstatic, international adventure poetry depicting the joys of living in the wilderness around the world beyond the confines of civilization; hence the name, *uncivilized ecstasies*.

In addition to writing insightful seasonal newsletters, Happyo's articles, quotes, videos, interviews, songs, and poems have been featured in dozens of renowned magazines, newspapers, other authors' books, and blogs. Due to being a powerful environmental leader, Happy's festival was infiltrated by pro-GMO secret corporate agents who attempted to destroy her festival, finances and reputation.

Having performed at more than 30 different major festivals in the USA, Happy is also sought-out speaker at expos, symposiums, churches, temples, yoga studios, retreats, webinars, cruise ships, and concert halls on an eclectic array of topics. Happyo frequently contributes to leading magazines and is often interviewed on a wide variety of internet, radio and television programs.

For Happy, "Every hour is happy hour". She feels grateful to be in service with a sincere aim to uplift humanity as she discovers the wonders of the world while welcoming guests home and roving with her beloved in an rv that they call "the creational vehicle". She asks, "Why recreate, when we can create?" For a fuller story of Happy's fun and fascinating life, plus books, articles, photos, videos, upcoming tours and events at her fairytale canyon retreat, *Heaven on Earth* (in a secret seasonal rainforest of northern Arizona!) please visit her at www.HappyOasis.com.

About the Coauthor (Yes, that's You!)

More Rave Reviews for *Bliss Conscious Communication*

"Fasten your blissbelt to receive tantalizing revelations of how to live as a dynamic pragmatic ecstatic! Happyo is waking up the world with the language of divine delight. "

—Wowza

"Shimmeringly transformative to the core, this book serves as a compelling invitation that dares us to live in ceaseless delight. The author creates a great case for the possibility of living contentedly and exuberantly all day long."

—Stella Diamond, founder of *Stella Diamond Yoga*

"An international treasure." — Ricki Burleigh, Wisdom-keeper

"Happyo is your personal guide to a world of unencumbered, uninhibited bliss-forward spectacularity. She will stop you in your tracks, guaranteed."

—Dave Weber, producer and engineer

"What a joyful riot and profound adventure it is to participate in the *Playshop For Blissologists* that accompanies this book. After the class, we received our *Certificates of Bliss* awarded by committing to coauthor the rest of our unique versions of this playfully-interactive book. Upon completing it, my brother and I were so delighted to be Certified Budding Blissologists that we framed and hung our diplomas in our offices. Happyo is an oasis of happiness; a kind-hearted, creative, bliss-filled, shining spirit dedicated to sharing uplifting language evocative of bliss. The loving frequency with which Happy laughs and lives is contagious. Be prepared to receive an upgrade in the Bliss Department and a first class passport gliding you into satchitananda - truth, consciousness and bliss."

—Meenakshi Angel Honig, acclaimed yogini, prolific author,
wellness consultant and Blissologist

"Promising and essential!"

—Brother Northstar, peripatetic poet and international peace pilgrim

"Happyo opens up new worlds of possibilities with her uplifting, infectiously love-of-life-affirming heart, inviting us to try on bigger, more beautiful, magical versions of our true selves."

> —Larisa Stow, musical leader of the Larisa Stow & Shakti Tribe Band

"Marvelously-inspiring to the soul! This outstanding journey dares us to rewrite the script of our lives into the most joyous existence imaginable. Every page is a courtship of the Divine, seducing us into a state of thriving. By illuminating the magic that comes from the words we use and the thoughts we think, Happyo helps us sculpt a masterpiece of communion with our highest selves."

> —Katrina Blair, author, educator and musician

"Happy Oasis has brought forth the Blissiplines for us to co-create a brighter world. *Bliss Conscious Communication* a treasure trove of easy techniques for making magic of everyday conversations."

> —Elijah Ray, singer and superconductor of the Band of Light

"Fabulous and insightful!"

> —Aleya Annaton, Emissary and author of *The Technology Of God*

"Happiness is our birthright. All rights reserved," reads the very first sentence of this book, immediately setting a tone of empowerment, pointing the way up toward glistening oneness hidden behind the diversity, thereby bringing us home to the realization that bliss conscious communion is an essential, joyful and ceaseless celebration."

> —Happyz, author of *Dreamz for the Awakened Soul*

"An ingenious, high-powered generator of gumption, gladness and generosity, this book especially appeals to those who aim to contribute to a more loving world as the author guides us to reconsider our relationship with language and each other."

> —Heidi Hohani, author of *Awaken Your Royalty*

"Very few things in life exceed our expectations. Hooray for *Bliss Conscious Communication*."
　　　　　　　　　　　　　　　　　　—George Parker, business manager

"Since taking the *"Playshop For Blissologist"*, becoming a Certified Budding Blissologist, and plunging into this *Bliss* book, it feels as if I've entered into a wonderful new world! My husband and I have been experimenting with these simple yet powerful bliss-invoking techniques. When a fellow briskly walked up to us today, quickly asked, *"How are you?"*, then whizzed by almost at a trot, my husband shouted out, *"What a wonderful question! Thank you for asking!"* The fellow stopped in his tracks. He turned and smiled at us, then came back to dive into a heartfelt conversation, thereby marking the start of a new friendship. This happened with several people today. These bliss tips are pragmatic, ecstatic, easy and fun. We can testify first hand that *Bliss Conscious Communication* offers a deeper, more consciously-loving way to authentically connect."
　　　　　　—Michelle Newman & Eliahu, Certified Blissologists

"Astonishingly heart-opening and astoundingly fun."
　　　　　　　　　　　　—Lisa Wade, president of ImpactAVillage.org and
　　　　　　　　　　　　　　co-author of *Journey of a Lost Boy of Sudan*

"Happy's infectious love of life is an inspiration. Our world would be a more harmonious place if we all adopt these *Bliss Conscious Communication* tools and suggestions.
　　—Scott Catamas, Emmy award-winning writer and loving communications coach

"Happyo lives and writes from her heart. She puts love into life, and life into love. Her bliss will become your bliss when you read and co-author the bliss within."
　　　　　　　　　　—Chef Mimi Kirk, vibrant vegan and longevity author

"What an efficacious transmission of enlightenment in a humorous and pragmatic way. This empowers us to ameliorate our lives and world with ease and pleasure by artfully, carefully and ease-fully choosing transformative vocabulary, starting with the ongoing conversations in our very own minds."
　　　　　　　　　　—Katharine Clark, health researcher & educator

"Completing the sublimely simple steps in this book will reveal how to be the inspirational life blood of your own conversations."

—Laura Lamun, the singing herbalist

"A deep sharing of unconditional love and a glorious adventure that demonstrates humanity's potential for conversational magnificence."

—Aeoliah Victory, recording artist, composer, author & visionary artist

"*Bliss Consious Communication* offers a blissful breakthrough in the art of communication, ushering in a paradigm shift in conversational communion that is not only effectual, meaningful and authentic, but also profoundly inspirational!"

—Ananda and Janaka, gardeners of the heart

"An inspiring emanation for loving spirits, Happyo is one of earth's natural wonders."

—Lynn Ericson, educator at a love-filled orphanage

"Ecstatic communication at it's blissful best. The delicious thought-provoking exercises inspire me and my loved ones to expand our ideas of who we truly are."

—Daniel Posney, web designer & healing artist

"Exhilarating and educative... Quantum energy fields beam from this ground-breaking book."

—Dr. Elizabeth Lambaer, youthologist, athlete & author of
Skinny Dipping In The Fountain Of Youth

"Masterfully draws out the love and childlike innocence inherent within us, based on the author's firsthand experience as an Adventure Anthropologist living with indigenous cultures. Happyo embodies vibrant health, radiant beauty and co-creation with the Divine in a way that connects us with our Higher Self. While participating in the *"Playshop for Blissologist"s*, I experienced the great joy generated choosing to use *Bliss Conscious Communication*. Even more so during this global shift of awakening, I enthusiastically recommend this heart-connecting book as well as the accompanying Playshops For Blissologists."

—Jerilee Camille, composer & herbalist

"Infinitely inspirational and creative, Happyo is a renaissance woman who has the unique ability to approach each day with optimism, and splendid cheer. Herein she gladly demonstrates with a grin how to be our own best Blissologist. The Blissipline endorphins within this book raise readers' spirits into heavenly highs. *Bliss Conscious Communication* is my daily trip to elation and the sutra of my soul."

—Sher Shah Khan, yogi & artist

"While learning *Bliss Conscious Communication* at a playshop, slowly, an illuminating light started shining within me, changing my perspective about how we communicate, inspiring me to live each moment with blissful presence. When we change our habits of communication, especially by transmuting what we say unconsciously into bliss-consciousness, we begin to awaken a seed that leads us to perceive, speak and live our divinity. This leads to states of happiness, joy and appreciation for all."

—Gissela Torrella, Columbian author of *Su Naturaleza Real* (Your True Nature)

"Happy Oasis is a great influence in my life as the hardest working peace-maker and bridge-maker I know, helping the world to be a better place to live. May you enjoy the bliss within."

—Wendy Daughtery, singer & songwriter

"A playfully insightful journey for the soul, brimming with unique, deliciously conscious, heart opening tools."

—Anahata Ananda, Shamangelic guide

"A magnificent journey into the heights of how we can create conversational heaven on earth. As Happy loves to say, "*Let's Bliss Forth with Love!*"

—Mia Margaret Angelica, angelic harpist & author of *Don't Worry, Be Happy*

If you enjoy this book,
you will likely love a playful poetry book of inspiration
and insightful international adventure anthropology
by Happy Oasis entitled *uncivilized ecstasies*.

Let's activate the miraculous.

May human kindness guide us.

The Beginning

Made in the USA
Monee, IL
05 August 2020